LLEWELLYN'S
CHAKRA ESSENTIALS SERIES

#1 • Root Chakra
JUNE 2023

#2 • Sacral Chakra
OCTOBER 2023

#3 • Solar Plexus Chakra
JUNE 2024

#4 • Heart Chakra
OCTOBER 2024

#5 • Throat Chakra
JUNE 2025

#6 • Third Eye Chakra
OCTOBER 2025

#7 • Crown Chakra
JUNE 2026

#8 • Out-of-Body Chakras
OCTOBER 2026

© Sweet Light Studio

Cyndi Dale is an internationally renowned author, speaker, and healer. She has written more than thirty books, including *Llewellyn's Complete Book of Chakras*; *Energy Healing for Trauma, Stress, and Chronic Illness*; *Kundalini*; and *The Complete Book of Chakra Healing*. Her year-long apprenticeship program through her company, Essential Energy, assists individuals in developing their natural intuitive and healing gifts. She also teaches in-depth classes via the Shift Network. Visit her at CyndiDale.com.

SOLAR PLEXUS CHAKRA

YOUR THIRD ENERGY CENTER
SIMPLIFIED + APPLIED

EDITED BY
CYNDI DALE

Llewellyn Publications
WOODBURY, MINNESOTA

FIRST EDITION
First Printing, 2024

Book design by Rebecca Zins
Cover design by Cassie Willett
Illustrations on pages 20, 107–109, and 117 by Llewellyn Art Department

Llewellyn Publications is a registered trademark of Llewellyn Worldwide Ltd.

Library of Congress Cataloging-In-Publication Data (pending)

ISBN 978-0-7387-7332-2

Llewellyn Publications
A Division of Llewellyn Worldwide Ltd.
2143 Wooddale Drive
Woodbury, MN 55125-2989
www.llewellyn.com
Printed in the United States of America

CONTENTS

List of Practices ... xiii

Introduction ... 1

PART 1: ESTABLISHING THE FOUNDATION OF YOUR THIRD CHAKRA KNOWLEDGE
[10]

1: Fundamentals ... 13

2: The Physical Side ... 43

3: Of the Psyche and the Soul ... 53

PART 2: APPLYING THIRD CHAKRA KNOWLEDGE IN REAL LIFE
[72]

4: Spirit Allies ... 77
MARGARET ANN LEMBO

5: Yoga Poses ... 91
AMANDA HUGGINS

6: Body Wisdom ... 105
LINDSAY FAUNTLEROY

7: Self-Healing and Grounding ... 119
   AMELIA VOGLER

8: Guided Meditations ... 131
   AMANDA HUGGINS

9: Vibrational Remedies ... 143
   JO-ANNE BROWN

10: Crystals, Minerals, and Stones ... 157
   MARGARET ANN LEMBO

11: Mantra Healing ... 167
   BLAKE TEDDER

12: Colors and Shapes ... 179
   GINA NICOLE

13: Recipes ... 191
   Part 1: ANTHONY J. W. BENSON, 191
   Part 2: SUSAN WEIS-BOHLEN, 199

   Conclusion ... 207

PRACTICES

Sounding the Universe Through Your
    Solar Plexus Bija ... 23

Be Red—As in the Fire Element ... 28

Relating to Your Vital Breath ... 32

Firing Up and Soothing the Kundalini
    in Your Third Chakra ... 38

Establish Connection Through Your Solar Plexus ... 61

Try on Your Third Chakra Archetypes ... 64

Mental Empathy: How to Interpret a Knowing ... 69

Setting a Third Chakra Intention ... 75

Kapalabhati Breathing ... 93

Full Yoga Flow to Activate the Third Chakra ... 96

Acupressure for Dynamic Energy Portals ... 107

Listen to Your Body via Your Inner Sun ... 109

Take a Lion's Breath ... 112

Fellowship with the Dandelion and Sunflower ... 113

Hakini Mudra Variation for Sunflowers ... 116

Balancing Your Third Chakra and Auric Field ... 122

Clearing the Solar Plexus with a Sun Walk ... 124

Grounding in the Integrity of You:
    A Solar Plexus Affirmation ... 127

Releasing Anger to Access Your Willpower ... 129

Clearing, Opening, and Charging the Third
    Chakra ... 134

Affirming Your Personal Power and Sense of
    Trust ... 137

The Sunny Day Meditation to Connect with
    Your Personal Power ... 139

Healing Sounds for the Solar Plexus Chakra ... 154

Create Your Own Third Chakra Vibrational
    Remedy ... 155

Stones for Self-Confidence, Mental Clarity,
    and Digestion ... 165

Start Simply with the Essence ... 172

Work with a Traditional Mantra ... 173

Intuiting a Personal Mantra ... 175

Attunement with Activated Fire ... 184

Activate Empowerment and Release Fear ... 185

INTRODUCTION

In your mind's eye, you peer at the sun. It is bright and gleaming, striking and bold. The world appears ready to burst into a thousand splinters of light. The way the brilliance seems to radiate sparkling and flaming jewels ... that's what the universe—and you—looks like through the lens of your third chakra. My code word for this chakra is "gemfire."

My term joins many other names for the third chakra, with chakras being defined as subtle energy centers that manage almost all aspects of your life.

Based in the stomach area, this energizing chakra is also called the navel or solar plexus chakra. "Solar" is a very apt label for your gemfire chakra, which is officially called *manipura* in Sanskrit, the origin of most traditional knowledge about chakras. Manipura means "shining sun" or "lustrous gem," and that's pretty much what this chakra, which is colored sun yellow (of course), is all about. When this center point is healthy, it illuminates your true self for all the world to see as well as produces a dazzling array of additional benefits that include worldly success, uplifting thoughts, access to your innate intelligence, the ability to strive willfully, healthy digestive processes, and so much more.

Lucky for you, this third subtle energy center is the topic of this book. It is also the third in an eight-book series called Llewellyn's Chakra Essentials.

Like all good storylines, this mini chakra series was initiated at square one with a book focused on your first chakra, also called the *muladhara*, or root, chakra. Found in your hip area, that brilliant red chakra, charged with supporting your physical health and assuring a secure life, is located underneath a spiffy orange chakra in your abdomen. Called the second or sacral chakra, the *svadhisthana* serves as a divining rod for creativity and emotions. Each book after this one will add yet another hue to your chakra collection, all the way to the eighth book, which features five out-of-body, or extraordinary, chakras. (More on those special chakras later.)

It doesn't matter if you read this book before its two predecessors or any book in the series before the other. Each book is a universe unto itself. That's because each of your chakras is a world of its own.

For context, it's important to know that all human (and most living) beings enjoy seven in-body chakras anchored in the central nervous system, which includes the spine and the brain. Their numerical ordering starts with the first chakra (at the base of the spine) and climbs upward to the seventh chakra (at the top of the head). In general, chakras are conduits for all life activities, also linking the mind, body, and soul. A very special type of spiritual matter, called *kundalini*, is known to rise from the first chakra and follow the flow of the chakras as well as interconnecting nerves. This divine energy enables better health and invites the experience of enlightenment. Your solar plexus chakra constitutes the third step of an awakened kundalini, which we'll further discuss in the first half of this book.

Regardless of whether this electrically charged and sacred "serpent power," as kundalini is often called, is winding through your system yet, your third chakra is a vital island of operation. On the simplest of levels, your third/gemfire chakra is a center of digestion, both physical and mental. I'll explain.

Within the churning cauldron of the manipura is found most of your digestive organs. Many of your neurological and immune functions are centered there as well. The body makes use of the third chakra's processes to break down and assimilate bodily nutrition as well as sort through and store ideas. Basically, beliefs—whether beneficial, harmful, or neutral—are cataloged and made operational within this chakra. These programs make all the difference in determining your sense of worth or lack thereof, which is foundational for both personal and professional empowerment.

Little wonder that yet another term for the third chakra is the "brain of the body." By working with the teachings and practices in this book, you'll improve not only the bodily functions of your third chakra but also your ability to intelligently accomplish your most dearly held life endeavors.

We're beholden to the ancient Hindus for the term *chakra*. The original language of the Indus Valley was Sanskrit, which used the word *chakra* to mean "spinning wheel of light." And chakras are all about light—the light of oneness within the self and a oneness with "the Spirit," or whatever name you use for a greater consciousness. This concept isn't only a Hindu one. Many cultures, including the traditional and contemporary Cherokee, Hopi, Hebrew, Mayan, Aztec, Berber, and African Kemetic, outline chakra-like centers and additional (albeit invisible) structures as the means to embody the vibrancy of love.

I want to take a moment to emphasize that, above all else, chakras are energy centers. Energy is information that moves, and spiritual masters have always asserted that we (and everything else) are composed of energy. It's exciting that modern science is now in agreement. The best way to portray how chakras work energetically is to picture them as stand-alone yet networked computers. The internal software within each chakra center grants access to its memory banks and lets the brain decipher what's going on in there.

There are two types of energy, however, and that distinction explains the importance of learning about—and interacting with—your chakras.

Physical energy makes up what is measurable in the everyday world. In the body, these concrete energies are managed by physical organs, channels, and fields, yet more than 99.999 percent of any object, including your body, is made of subtle energy.[1] While it's certainly important to get in touch with—and improve the function of—your physical structures, the truth is that these systems are largely organized by subtle energies and their corresponding structures.

There are three main structures that manage both subtle and many physical energies. Chakras, comparable to the physical organs, act like the boss. There are also subtle channels and fields that make up the other two systems within the subtle energy anatomy, which is also often called the subtle body.

It's a lot to take in. However, because understanding your third chakra will overlap with knowledge of the subtle channels and fields, I'm going to continue your subtle anatomy lesson for a couple more paragraphs.

There are two main types of subtle channels. These are your meridians and the nadis.

1   Ali Sundermier, "99.9999999% of Your Body Is Empty Space," Sciencealert, September 23, 2016, https://www.sciencealert .com/99-9999999-of-your-body-is-empty-space.

Meridians flow through the connective tissue and carry subtle energies throughout the body. The term stems from traditional Chinese medicine, although these channels are also portrayed in other traditions around the world. The label *nadis* is Hindu in origin. These channels are equivalent to your nerves. Many of the body's thousands of nadis interact directly with the seven in-body chakras, as do the meridians.

As well, each chakra creates its own field of subtle energy, called an *auric field* or *auric layer*. Together, these individual and encircling spheres form the entire auric field. Each layer serves as a protective barrier, energetically selecting which energies enter or exit based on the programming within its correlated chakra. In this book we'll be examining the third auric layer or field since it's the extension of your third chakra.

Now, you've already noticed—based on my preemptive declaration that there is an eighth book in this series—that I teach a system of twelve chakras and auric fields. There are many reasons I do this, starting with the fact that I perceived twelve chakras and auric fields when I was a child.

I didn't know at the time, of course, that the colorful balls or streams of light I saw within and around people were all about subtle energy. My parents were Protestant. As I often admit, we were White Wonder Bread Norwegian Lutherans, and there were no lesson plans in Sunday school about chakras. Nonetheless, the rainbow orbs and fields I saw around people, plants, and animals—and the beautiful hues of red, orange, yellow, and more—were as real to me as the lefse and lutefisk (Norwegian foods, all white) my mother served at the holidays. There were twelve of those emanating multicolored balls and rays of pigment. I could see them with my everyday eyes but also with my inner viewfinder.

Starting in my twenties, I began interacting with healers, shamans, intuitives, and gurus from around the world. They also knew about the various subtle energy structures. Over the years I've discovered that certain science disciplines do too. I was shocked to find out that there is really nothing imperative about working with only seven chakras, the model used in the West since the early 1900s. The truth is that chakra-based and other spiritual medicine systems from around the world have depicted anywhere from three to dozens of chakras.

Since my first book featuring my twelve-chakra system was published through Llewellyn years ago, my depiction has become internationally renowned. In addition to the standard seven chakras, there are five additional chakras, which are outside of the body proper. There is a reason that the extraordinary five chakras are so popular: interacting with them greatly enhances the ability to understand and formulate the small and big miracles that are our birthright. That is why you'll learn all about these five out-of-body chakras in the eighth book in this series.

Now that I've taken you on a brief detour, let's return to the third chakra leg of your trek.

There are two parts to this book. I am the sole author of part 1, which consists of three chapters that cover the basics about your solar plexus/gemfire chakra. Much of the information originates from the classical Hindu bed of knowledge, although I deviate into modern ideas when it's beneficial. Interspersed are a few practices to help you personalize the material.

The first chapter features third chakra nuts and bolts, including data about the solar plexus chakra's overarching purpose and its location, names, color, and sound. I'll also discuss the associated elements, breaths, lotus petals, and affiliated god and goddess.

In chapter 2 I'll treat you to in-depth knowledge of the physical nature of your manipura chakra. Like all chakras, your solar plexus chakra is rooted within its own region of your spine and linked to an endocrine gland and other bodily areas. After outlining the physical systems managed by your third chakra, I'll then provide examples of the disease processes that might occur if this chakra is imbalanced. I'll close out part 1 in chapter 3 by delving into the psychological and spiritual functions of your solar plexus chakra. Then it's time to start the real fun. Part 2 is all about doing, centered on this statement:

You can create your best life by excavating and applying the energies of your third chakra.

I'll kick off part 2 with rousing introductory material about intention that will constitute your foremost healing and manifesting tool from this point forward. You'll also participate in a guided meditation aimed at assisting you with feeling into your third chakra. And then you'll meet new friends.

Every chapter in part 2 is authored by an energy expert. Via the first of these specialists, you'll meet your spiritual allies. The next expert will stretch you into third chakra yoga poses. That's just the beginning. By the time you're done with part 2, you'll have acquired a rich toolkit of third chakra practices that includes the use of guided meditation, vibrational remedies, stones, sounds, shapes, colors, spirit allies, yoga poses, grounding exercises, and even recipes to boost your solar plexus functions.

As I hope has become apparent, there are many reasons to process within—and polish up—your manipura chakra. In fact, there are as many motives as there are facets on your amazing gemfire chakra.

PART 1

ESTABLISHING THE FOUNDATION
OF YOUR THIRD CHAKRA KNOWLEDGE

• • • • • •

Set both hands on the front side of your solar plexus. Inhale deeply, feeling your stomach extend. Exhale completely, noticing the concave movement. As you continue inhaling and exhaling, visualize this area of your body as shining yellow and pay attention to whatever arises in your mind.

Let those thoughts float across your inner mind screen, no matter how many there are. When you're ready to clear them, simply intensify the brilliant sunshine within your solar plexus area. Watch intuitively as the radiating rays swiftly sweep up those thoughts and release them into the air, where they will be transformed by nature.

It is amazing to feel less stressed.

You have just interacted with your third chakra. Also called your solar plexus chakra, this potent subtle energy center governs mental activities, belief systems, personal and professional power, and many functions necessary to bodily well-being. As a baseline, within this center you're provided the ability to separate functional ideas from dysfunctional ones. Once you choose to operate only from the former, this chakra evolves into the fiery gemstone that it really is. Through that lens of higher truth, everything you think or do automatically achieves a singular goal: to guarantee that you compose the concertos of goodness you're uniquely here to create.

In this section of the book, I'm going to build a roadway of data. Brick by brick, the information within will help you comprehend the facts about your third chakra you'll need in order to assure that you can bolster its effectiveness physically, psychologically, and spiritually, the main objectives of part 1. In the first chapter, I'll chiefly focus on the knowledge inherited from Hindu culture, tossing in a few salient points from modern times. I'll also return to the topic of kundalini that was raised in the introduction.

Chapter 2 forms the skeleton upon which I'll flesh out the physical nature of your solar plexus chakra. After revisiting the topic of kundalini again, we'll then charge forth into chapter 3, which will highlight the psychological and spiritual qualities of your third chakra. Like jewels gleaming atop an altar, the practices strewn throughout these three chapters will help you begin to experience the glittering features of this chalice of truth and love.

1

FUNDAMENTALS

Reflect upon how much of your life is spent thinking. We humans are thinking creatures. We all know, however, that the quality of most thoughts is quite questionable.

Welcome to your third chakra, your central storage container of the thoughts, ideas, and concepts you have collected to date. The ideas that underlie your perceptions and actions have so many sources that it is hard to keep track of them. In fact, you've accrued those ideas from other lifetimes as well as from your ancestors, family of origin, and culture. You've also arrived at more than a few core beliefs through your own experiences. One of the reasons it's so important to acquire the foundational teachings about your third chakra is that once you understand them, you'll automatically begin sorting helpful from harmful thoughts. By the time you're ready to assume only higher truths as your modus operandi, you'll be able to embrace the type of personal and professional success and physical well-being the third chakra is charged with facilitating.

In this chapter, I'll first provide a real-life story about the capabilities of the third chakra. You'll then find several mini sections that will further drill down into your gem-fire chakra education. Most of the information derives from Hindu traditions, which means that it has been developed over thousands of years in various Eastern cultures. Some of the insights will be more modern so you can better apply the material when it's time to do that. Also included is an in-depth discussion about kundalini, the sacred divine energy that is often considered to originate from the first chakra—except when it's considered to be formulated in the third chakra. To assist you in embracing these fundamentals so you can begin to better your everyday life right now, I'll also present several practices.

Let's get going; it's time for you to shine even more brightly than you already do.

THE ESSENCE OF YOUR THIRD CHAKRA

Eva began seeing me because she had been struggling with digestive issues for years. She is not alone. Digestive conditions cause 25 percent of all surgeries in America. They have clearly become one of the nation's most serious health problems, including the loss of workplace hours. This problem only grows year after year.

From a chakra point of view, one of the major subtle energy centers underlying gastrointestinal problems is the third chakra. Of course, it's a hotbed for other challenges as well, including low self-esteem, self-hatred, lack of empowerment, a racing mind, negative self-talk, discriminatory viewpoints, career challenges, and an inability to organize—or its reverse: being overly analytical.

I'm not a doctor or a therapist. I'm an energy healer, and I draw upon my intuition to assist clients in accessing their own inner knowledge. What makes my job unique is that I can often perceive the connecting dots between a person's physical and spiritual aspects. In other words, I read frequencies, the bands of energies that compose the chakras and other subtle energy structures. The frequencies that compose the third chakra deal with our foundational belief systems and often destructive ways they affect our lives.

I easily guessed that Eva's physical issues correlated with her third chakra. Most of our digestive organs, including the liver, pancreas, stomach, spleen, gallbladder, and much of the small intestine, are situated within its domain. Apropos of the third chakra, Eva also complained of incessant mental chatter, most of it full of self-loathing comments, and a fear of standing up for herself on the job. Over the last few years, she'd watched one coworker after another earn promotions while she sat parked on the same rung of the ladder, even though she was often doing much of the others' work.

Eva was willing to consult with a therapist and a gastro-intestinal specialist while working with me. My job was to explore her symptoms to find their causes and shift them energetically.

Two situations from childhood stood out. First, her mother, an alcoholic, frequently attacked Eva and her sister with abusive statements. Second, whenever her mother was on a drinking tear, her father would prepare the meals, whereas normally her mother did. Eva appreciated his effort but couldn't help making a face every time. His lack of culinary expertise meant that many of their dinners and packed school lunches were borderline inedible. Basically, Eva and her sister were malnourished despite being raised in a middle-class family.

I assisted Eva with uncovering the feelings related to the obvious neglect and verbal and emotional abuse, as did her therapist. My major contribution to Eva's welfare, however, involved showing her how her parents had impacted her energetically.

Even silent messages, such as the self-destructive ones that Eva's mother and father kept to themselves, project psychic impressions into those who are exposed to them. Especially when we're young and vulnerable, we become saturated with others' inner thoughts. As we grow up, these become the standard for our self-esteem and self-confidence. Basically, Eva was carrying the same negative prototypes that characterized the poor self-worth and lack of self-love in her parents as well as her grandparents, who were also either addicts or codependent to addicts.

Eva kept her deeply rooted self-hatred to herself, refusing to say boo to anyone else for fear of turning out like her mom, so her thoughts festered. To compensate, she developed a flair for perfectionism, which is frequently the case with third chakra problems.

The years spent being undernourished didn't help. It's hard to assert personal power when you don't feel well physically, and Eva hardly ever felt strong enough to deal with her issues, much less press forward in life.

Over time, Eva started to break free from the internal loop of self-criticism. She learned to accept her mistakes and share her needs, as well as successes, with the people around her. Though she credited both me and her therapist with helping her pinpoint her emotions, she stated that she gained the most assistance from using the types of techniques you'll discover in this book; these involved clearing the harmful subtle energies that had been imploded into her third chakra. Her active involvement in the energetic aspects of her history and present-day life made it all the easier for her medical professional to uncover the physical reasons for her malabsorption issues. After a naturopath put her on a customized diet, Eva experienced exponential physical and personal growth. She left her workplace, which would only budge so far to accommodate her happier and more hale self, and today she runs her own vibrant business.

When the beliefs within our third chakra are realistic—meaning positive and loving—all parts of our life respond with an upswing. What we hold dear internally will assist us in thriving externally. In tune with our true calling, we'll eagerly establish the protocols necessary to set and meet our goals. We'll also have great fun smelling the roses along the way.

By the way, Eva also took up gardening. She figured out that life really isn't just about working.

Now that Eva's story has shone upon a few of the facets of the third chakra, it's time to embrace more details.

Overarching Purpose

Manipura is the energy center of personal and professional power, mental activity, self-esteem, and willpower. It is so powerful that it deserves the label of gemfire chakra.

IT'S ALL IN THE NAME:
TERMS FOR THE THIRD CHAKRA

The Sanskrit name for the third chakra can be broken into two parts. *Mani* means jewel or gem; *pura* means dwelling place. Thus, it can be translated as "city of gems."

LOCATION OF THE THIRD CHAKRA

This chakra is found in the solar or gastric plexus, in the part of the vertebral column behind our stomach area (see page 20). You can find the top side of it by putting a hand right below your breasts. Its effect radiates seven centimeters (just under three inches) above and below your navel. If you are feeling stressed, you may be able to feel this nerve plexus as a tight knot just below your sternum.

COLOR OF THE THIRD CHAKRA

Each chakra functions on a different set of frequencies. Frequencies are organized into bandwidths that are recognized as specific ranges of colors and sounds. I'll discuss the sound of your solar plexus chakra in the next section.

In terms of color, your third chakra serves the subtle energies in the yellow spectrum. Right below it lies your second chakra, which operates in the orange zone; below that is your first chakra, which is all about red. Yellow is considered the hue of wisdom and intellect.

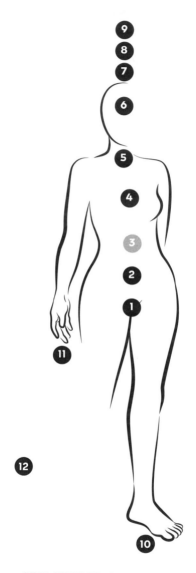

THE TWELVE-CHAKRA SYSTEM

The second or sacral chakra, which is orange, is a mix of the red of the first chakra and the yellow of the third chakra; red and yellow create orange. The second chakra produces our basic feelings—anger, fear, sadness, disgust, and joy. You could say that these are a composite of the raw survival instincts in the first chakra and the beliefs held in the third chakra. Put all these together and you arrive at emotions. Emotions are a mix of at least one feeling (or awareness) and one belief, and they formulate the "energy of motion." Hence you can see how chakras are independent but also interdependent.

You'll learn ways to interact with colors to cleanse and enhance your third chakra in chapter 12.

Yellow is known as an invigorating color, stimulating our nerves and glands and moving us into physical activity. It makes us more alert and can even boost our memory, which makes sense as it is the hue of the chakric "brain of the body."[2] Its association with the sun in all parts of the world encourages us to feel warmed and happy, able to create the best of all possible futures. At times it is also associated with fear and cowardice. As with anything in life, it is up to us to choose how to apply the third chakra's capability.

---

2   Kate Smith, "Color Symbolism & Meaning of Yellow," Sensational Color, https://www.scnsationalcolor.com/meaning-of-ycllow/.

One ultimate goal is to move out of weakness and prejudice and toward empowerment and goodwill.

SOUND OF THE THIRD CHAKRA

The Hindus believed that tones are held within the chakras. These are called *bijas* (seed sounds). Other labels for these inner sounds are *bija mantras* (master sounds). When repeated, a mantra is a sound that initiates a meditative state. When employing your third chakra, you're encouraged to chant with its specific bija/seed sound to invite the desired change. You'll learn how to do this in chapter 11 with Blake Tedder's expertise.

In contemporary spiritual circles, the solar plexus chakra has become related to the E note. It is the third step of a sequence that begins with a C in the first chakra, moves to D in the second chakra, and proceeds accordingly.

Traditional Hindus assigned the sound *Ram* to this sunshine chakra, pronounced "rum" when chanting it.

This seed syllable is linked to a god and goddess (whom you'll meet in greater depth later in this chapter) within the Hindu pantheon. The god is Rudra. He grants wishes and dispels fears. This means that when uttering *Ram*, you can activate the same potentials within your third chakra. The goddess is Lakini. She and Rudra perform many of the same tasks.

SOUNDING THE UNIVERSE THROUGH YOUR SOLAR PLEXUS BIJA

As the brain of the body, your third/gemfire chakra is often considered the source of words, which makes it particularly responsive to sound. To experience the accuracy of this statement, try this practice.

Place your thumb on your navel and say a word out loud. Pay attention and you will sense the vibration of the sound before it emanates from your lips. The vibration starts in the navel, rises to the larynx, and is then produced as audible sound.

Besides using the bija mantra *Ram*, you can also repeat the mantra *Om shanti* to clear your solar plexus and make crystal clear the messages you deliver to the world. *Om* is the original sound of the Divine, and *shanti* means "peace."

Yet another beautiful mantra is this one:

Om mani padme hum

This mantra means "Praise to the jewel in the lotus" or "My adoration to the master of the jeweled city." The vibrations of this mantra free us from inner tensions and activate manipura's potential.

SOUND CARRIER

Every chakra is associated with a unique being that is thought to carry the sound of that chakra. The sound carrier of the third chakra is a ram (as in the animal, not the seed syllable). The ram promotes spiritual qualities, imparting virtues such as strength, wisdom, and bravery. The vehicle of the fire god Agni, it depicts our third chakra qualities, promoting steadfastness and the refusal to give up.

Think about the inner nature—and outer actions—of a ram. This animal reflects a surge in mentality and our response to inspiration. It is also able to penetrate, overcome, and direct its willpower to achieve a breakthrough. Let yourself wonder what might occur if you devote yourself to these same faculties. Allow yourself to be infused with ideas, and then create and follow a plan to its completion. That truly is the key to success in any endeavor.

LOTUS PETALS AND APPEARANCE

Lotus petals are a traditional stylization to describe all in-body chakras. In fact, every chakra has a different number and color of petals.

From a subtle energy standpoint, the petals depict the swirling motion of a chakra. Chakras absorb, process, and release the subtle energies related to their band of frequencies. They also produce and interrelate with physical energies that run within this same frequency spectrum, which means that they are impacted by the movements of the physical organs, fluids, sound waves, and electromagnetic field (EMF) activity in their localized area, as well as all the subtle energies they react to from inside and outside of a being. If you were to freeze the whirling energies of a chakra, you would see a picture of a vortex with several outstretching arms of EMF. Those arms would appear like the petals of a lotus flower.

By musing upon the lotus of a particular chakra, you sink into that chakra's enlightenment qualities. In Hindu culture, the lotus represents the spiritual life. Lotuses are rooted in muddy water even as their blossoms reach toward the sun. What is murky below becomes clear above; what a testimony to life. Water itself is considered the *maya* (illusion) of life, so the petals could be seen to represent our true selves. How fitting for the third chakra, where the evidence of what is occurring deep within us is made apparent in our life successes.

Manipura has ten blue petals, which are as blue as the center of a super-hot flame. This makes the chakra both constructive and destructive. Letters on the petals are pham, dam, dham, nam, tam, tham, dam, dham, nam, and pam. These petals indicate the following obstacles to reform: spiritual ignorance, treachery, jealousy, shame, delusion, disgust, fear, foolishness, thirst, and sadness.

THIRD CHAKRA SYMBOLS:
THE YANTRAS

A *yantra* is a geometric diagram. As such, yantras have been employed for over 13,000 years in Indian culture to aid in meditation. Most yantras represent specific gods and goddesses. As a devotee, when you focus on a yantra symbol—whether it is depicted visually on paper or within your mind—you are said to receive healing and insight from the related deity. Yantras can also serve to remind you of a specific task or vow, perhaps one you believe you must keep in this lifetime to achieve your spiritual purpose or express your genuine self.

Your third chakra's yantra is a downward-pointing triangle within a bright yellow circle. Ten dark blue or black petals surround the circle. Standing at the midpoint of each side of the triangle and reaching out toward the circle is a T shape that serves as a doorway. Together, these T shapes form a type of swastika, a Sanskrit symbol for well-being and universal welfare.

We are not talking about the Nazi swastika when employing the third chakra symbol. For decades, yoga experts have tried to explain that the Nazis didn't use the true swastika, which is part of many cultures, including those of the Cherokee, Greeks, Druids, and non-Hindu religions, including Buddhism. Instead, the Nazis employed a hooked cross. The Nazi swastika shows the arms at 45 degrees, making the symbol slant, and they made additional changes to the ancient icon, while the swastika of Hinduism portrays the basc arm as flat. One modern swastika expert believes that Hindu society considered the swastika to serve Vedic mathematics in its representation of "the fourth stage of consciousness, which is beyond waking, sleeping and dreaming."[3]

Overall, consider the swastika as denoting good luck. Within the third chakra it emphasizes the nature of fire, which is to rise and transform.

GROSS ELEMENT

According to many religions, including Hinduism, matter is composed of several different elements. In Eastern religions it is thought that there are four basic elements: earth, water, fire, and wind (or air). Some systems also endorse a fifth element: space. In Hinduism, the gross/major element of the third chakra is fire.

3 Kalpana Sunder, "The Ancient Symbol that was Hijacked by Evil," BBC Culture, August 16, 2021, https://www.bbc.com/culture/article/20210816-the-ancient-symbol-that-was-hijacked-by-evil.

Fire relates to the Hindu theory that digestion is accomplished through heat; both food and ideas are burned to formulate vital energy. It is often used in Hindu ceremonies to signify a rite of passage, such as birth, marriage, or death.[4]

Color of the Gross Element

Think of the various colors of fire. There are many, including the yellow of the sun that is the broad or cumulative depiction of the third chakra. The element of fire itself, however, is fire red, which is one of the reasons I like to call this the gemfire chakra.

As a sun chakra, your solar plexus center is served by the heat of the flame-red element. Within it we digest ideas and nourishment, turning them into mental and body heat, respectively. Cosmic energy, such as that formulating higher truths and awareness, can also be considered a sort of flame.

PRACTICE

BE RED—AS IN THE FIRE ELEMENT

As I've shared, red is the color of the third chakra's gross element. Red provides energy and enthuses your mind and

4   Richard Oldale, "The Importance of Fire in Hinduism," Antaryami, September 25, 2017, https://www.antaryami.com/hindu-mythology/the-importance-of-fire-in-hinduism/.

actions. It is dynamic and exciting, revealing and empowering your desires while providing the fuel needed to go after a goal. Its passionate nature also tells you when you are in danger, waving the red flag that says *stop* when necessary.

Are you in search of the qualities of red right now?

If so, breathe deeply. Focus on the circumstances related to the situation in your mind and put both hands on your solar plexus, the center of your third chakra. Now picture the flames of red present within this chakra. Give permission for any hues necessary to be awakened and spread. Observe how many different hues of red arise in your vision. Embrace the shades, hues, and intensities that are available to you. It's okay if other colors present themselves too. Red is a primary color and often activates other parts of the rainbow.

If any specific issue you've been facing comes to mind, allow it to present itself. Watch and feel as the wash of reds consumes this issue, performing a beautiful sort of alchemy. Now, every time you inhale, any subtle energy necessary will enter and fuel the bowl of reds within your third chakra. As well, every exhalation will release the subtle frequencies that have been causing stress.

As red as Agni, the sun god, and as brilliant as the rising or setting sun, release the process and your hands when you feel complete. Go forward into your life shining and clean.

PREDOMINANT SENSE AND SENSE ORGAN

Every one of the seven in-body chakras is matched with a sense and a sensory organ. There are many reasons why it's so important to know this.

It's tempting to perceive chakras as only subtle, or immaterial. The truth is that every chakra located within and even outside the body helps manage the physical self. As an example, each chakra supervises a specific sense and the organ that relates to it. The sense associated with manipura is sight, and the sense organ is the eye.

Sight is one of our most vital senses. Consider how often you rely on your external vision to gather data, take in the world, and make decisions. It might not immediately make sense to think of sight as emanating from your gut.

You make decisions about what foods to select based on visuals. You also judge the character of a stranger via your eyes. The ability to see and evoke memories that enable us to interpret what we view is laid throughout the body. Given that the third chakra is a central way station for our neurology and inner knowing, it's logical to surmise that this chakra is linked with sight and eyes.

You can take advantage of the association between your navel chakra and eyesight in several ways. One is to undertake an experiment. Decide to abstain from forming a verdict about a food, person, culture, news article, or personal event based on your viewpoint. Instead, assess with your gut. Let your solar plexus chakra inform your mind and see what happens.

ACTION ORGAN

Every chakra is associated with an action organ. This is a bodily area that brings physical energy into that chakra and keeps it motivated and bolstered. The action organ for the third chakra is the anus.

Your anus is at the farthest region of your digestive tract. Through it, stools leave your body. It is a fitting organ for the third chakra if you return to the knowledge that the chakra is basically about the digestion of ideas and nutrition. Whatever doesn't suit you—mentally or physically—is metaphorically and actively passed out through your anus.

VITAL BREATH

In Hinduism, the most vital life force is called *prana*. This is a very real yet ethereal energy that moves through all living beings. It assures vibration, activity, and our very lives. It is also called spirit breath, breath of life, and the vital principle. Prana interpenetrates all aspects of reality and is considered a subtle energy. The gross or obvious manifestation of prana is the breath.

There are five different types of prana, which are also called *vayus* (winds). The third chakra is associated with one of these vital breaths, the *samana*. Samana controls the digestive fire and enables digestion. It aids the absorption and assimilation of nutrients and supports metabolism. Because this vital breath is related to fire, it also purifies and supports strong mental activity.

PRACTICE

RELATING TO YOUR VITAL BREATH

As shared above, your third chakra's vital breath is samana. The fire nature of this breath aids in digestion and purification. To experience the consolidating force of samana, you can enjoy this short exercise.

Focus your mind on your navel area and call upon the transformative energy of fire that lies inherent within it. You are actively awakening the energy of samana, which is made of life energies that rise from below and fall from above. As samana is activated within your third chakra, let yourself experience its balancing effect. While it cleanses negative thoughts and bodily toxins, it also stabilizes the center part of your body. You can now approach life in a more regulated and ease-filled way.

ATTRIBUTE

An attribute is a quality. Each in-body chakra is affiliated with a specific and special quality that is related to its sound carrier. As per your third chakra, your sound carrier is the ram, which provides you with the qualities of achievement and supremacy. We all have times we need to be brave and persevere. Your inner ram will enable just that.

RULING GODDESS

Lakini Shakti, also known as Bhadra Kali, is the primary goddess associated with your third chakra. She is a compassionate form of Kali, the ferocious goddess. Her three faces reflect the scope of vision employed by the third chakra. In her four arms she holds a thunderbolt, an arrow, fire, and a mudra that grants boons and cancels fear. She can be called upon for many other reasons as well—as many as are reflected in the gem facets of the third chakra jewel.

RULING GOD

Manipura's associated god is Rudra, also called Old Shiva. This is the wrathful form of Shiva, who represents the power of destruction. His name comes from the root *rud*, which means "crying," signifying the lamentation of endings. He is red with anger but also white or gray because his body is covered with ashes. He sits on a tiger skin and is also dressed in one, and he holds a trident and a drum. Adorned with snakes, he dispels both fear and anger. We can use his modeling to control our more violent tendencies while using the power of destruction in a wise way, such as to protect an innocent or end a harmful pattern.

RULING PLANET

Your solar plexus/gemfire chakra is ruled by the sun, a force supportive of individuality and self-expression. In most cultures, the sun occupies a very important place in ideology and achieving life's very real needs. It symbolizes the energy needed to grow and be clear, confident, and positive. Often depicted in a circle, it can also relate to wholeness, selfhood, and a manifestation of divinity.

RELATED AURIC FIELD

The auric field for the solar plexus chakra is the third auric layer. In the twelve-chakra system, the third auric field is found about eight to ten inches away from the skin.

This third auric field is programmed by the ideas held within your third chakra. Those ideas or beliefs are a collection of ancestral experiences and your ancestors' conclusions about them. They are also influences from your own childhood and family of origin, life experiences and your ideas about them, and cultural and societal norms. Some of the third auric field programs consist of negative beliefs, but these can be transformed into uplifting and loving truths by cleansing and healing the third chakra. By doing this, you can learn how to better love yourself, show your attributes and personal power to the world, and draw opportunities that can yield success. Then use the practices in this book to alter the programs in your third chakra and get ready for more fun.

YOUR SECONDARY SOLAR PLEXUS CHAKRAS

There are two main secondary chakras associated with your third chakra. The first is the *surya* chakra, which is also called the *hrit* chakra. My favorite term for it—and what I call it—is the celestial wishing tree. This beautiful secondary chakra, typically found on the left side of the body in relation to the solar plexus, is believed to help you link to the Spirit through prayer. In turn, the Spirit is open to answering your deepest and most heartfelt desires.

The surya chakra is also considered to provide your third chakra with the element of heat. In Tibetan Buddhism this chakra is called the fire wheel because of this relationship.

The other chakra frequently associated with manipura is *manas* or the mind chakra. It is usually located between the heart and the navel, close to surya and sometimes above the sixth chakra (on the forehead). When found in the lower part of the body, it is linked to five sense objects plus the mind. On the forehead it is depicted with six petals. In Tibetan Buddhism it has six spokes, is called the wind wheel, and is found on the forehead.

DOES KUNDALINI START IN MANIPURA?

Kundalini is a divine energy that runs upward through the spine to cleanse your subtle and physical body and stairstep you toward enlightenment.

In Hinduism it is considered a form of divine feminine energy, and on the physical level, it relates to the electricity that keeps every cell, organ, and organ system healthy and pumping with life. The word *kundalini* in Sanskrit means "coiled snake," and that is how it is often pictured: a red serpent unfurling from the first/root chakra, located near the coccyx, rising upward through your nadis. These are the subtle energy channels that relate to your nerves. In its climb, the serpent or red kundalini can bring catastrophe as it triggers your physical and psychological issues, but it also can bring the type of divine grace needed to love yourself and learn how to live in an awakened, kind state.

According to Buddhist theory as well as many tantric texts, kundalini activation starts in the third chakra, not the first, as is commonly thought. The thinking is that the previous two chakra stopping points, the first and second chakras, are higher realms of our animal selves, while human consciousness begins at the solar plexus region and becomes refined as kundalini energy moves upward.

Because the third chakra is of a higher order than the ones below it, many practitioners believe that reaching the third chakra during a kundalini rising secures a fail-safe environment. Sincere aspirants cannot fall back down the ladder; their consciousness now can only rise. Still other practitioners believe that kundalini is more like a vertical accordion and can slip all the way back to the root chakra in the hips from any perch, including from the crown chakra, which lies at the top of the head.

Whether or not your solar plexus chakra is truly fail-safe, it plays a significant role in the rising of the kundalini. It is certain that several forms of *prana* (the cosmic collection of the five vital forces) use the solar plexus as a conjunction point. Within the solar plexus, you can work through your inherited issues and open to life's goodness as if with the wings of an angel.

Traditionally, *pranayama* (breathing exercises) serve as vital tools to assist with the control of the major pranas. When an aspirant's issues are cleared—when higher consciousness is achieved—the vital force of the third chakra, samana, moves from the periphery of the body into the core. This implosion can spark an upward rise, like providing fuel for a rocket.

It can feel incredible to achieve calm and kundalini at the same time. The following breathing exercise will accomplish this goal.

FIRING UP AND SOOTHING THE KUNDALINI IN YOUR THIRD CHAKRA

Your third chakra is like a sun, a center in which energy bursts into being as kundalini joins together various forms of prana. To enable this process, as well as reduce potential danger from the resulting combustion, I recommend using the *mrigi* mudra to breathe through the right nostril alone. That nostril is your sun nostril, inviting the fire of new life and purification into your system. (In contrast, the left nostril is your lunar nostril, which invites calm and peace.)

The right nostril links with the pingala nadi, one of three main *nadis* (nerve pathways) associated with kundalini. Your spine is the main nadi. The ida nadi is a feminine and serene nadi, linked with your right brain and receptive qualities. The pingala nadi is associated with the left-brain hemisphere and your rational, logical mind as well as masculine, verbal, and physical activities. The pingala nadi matches with the right nostril as both are solar in nature, increasing bodily heat and acidic secretions.

For those of you who are nervous system nerds, the spine is considered your central and balanced pathway. The ida is linked to the parasympathetic nervous system, which provides "rest and digest" traits, and the pingala is associated with your sympathetic nervous system, which drives you forward.

We naturally switch between left and right nostrils during the day, with the most precise transition at dawn and dusk. To deliberately use only the right nostril is to emphasize chakras that are fiery in nature, such as the third. This exercise will also help you with activities related to the third chakra such as working hard, writing, debating, and undergoing spiritual practices.

> » To perform right nostril breathing, sit in a comfortable position, block your left nostril with one or two fingers, and then inhale through your right nostril. Breathe in through the right nostril and exhale through the left for one to three minutes. You can spend less time at this practice if you feel too stressed— simply back off and breathe through only your left nostril until you feel calmer.

CELESTIAL PLANE
OF THE THIRD CHAKRA

There are chakras and realms of existence that lie below your first chakra. The planes that are linked to a cosmic realm are called *lokas*. These look like luminous spheres and describe various levels of existence. Through the third chakra we link to *svar loka*, a celestial or heavenly plane that is considered to be between the sun and the pole star. Through this plane we connect to the devas in Hinduism.

SUMMARY

This bright yellow chakra is your center of personal power and willpower; it is also, appropriately, the home of the red fire element. Located in the solar plexus and linked to the solar plexus vertebrae, it is also associated with the pancreas and regulates the organs in that area. Its action organ is the anus, and it is also associated with your eyes and the sense of light. It is here that we relate to the Hindu devas found in the celestial plane of *svar loka*, and we access hidden powers as well as gifts such as mental empathy.

Symbolized by a downward triangle within a circle, this ten-petaled chakra helps us gain achievement and defeat the inclination to be supreme. Its sound, *Ram*, is carried by a four-footed ram and the goddess Lakini Shakti. Along with the god Rudra, this goddess uses the sun's energy to help you manage your life. Activated while you're young, this chakra assists you with deciding how to interact with the world.

Now that you've considered the fundamentals of your third chakra, it's time to excavate the physicality of this flame-like gemstone chakra.

2

THE PHYSICAL SIDE

Your arms, the chair you're sitting in, the food you ate this morning—all these things are made of physical energy. Yet even though they all seem quite solid, most of the energy in these seemingly concrete objects is subtle. The same is true of things you can't objectively touch, hear, or view—like thoughts, hopes, and dreams. Regardless of the predominance of subtle energy, it's essential to discuss the physicality of a thing, such as your third chakra.

Ahh, that solar plexus chakra. Its physical contributions to your well-being are significant. For one, most of your digestive organs sit within this area. As such, it assures that your body and your life activities are constantly animated. It is also implicitly bound to your neurological and immune functioning and so many other health factors. As we examine the physiology of your gemfire chakra in this chapter, consider making a promise like this one to yourself:

*I vow to support my third chakra to better
sustain all aspects of my physical self.*

You'll learn just how practical that commitment can be.

OVERVIEW OF THE THIRD CHAKRA'S PHYSICAL REACH

Your third chakra is rooted in the solar plexus region, on both the front and back sides of the body. Physically, this area is tasked with busily energizing your cells, organs, organ systems, and so much more.

This chakra is grounded in the celiac nerve plexus, located in the region of the vertebrae near your kidneys. Its influence expands throughout your entire solar plexus area and encompasses most of your digestive organs. As with all chakras, the third chakra has a major endocrine gland—in this case, the pancreas—which is charged with governing the entire part of the body that emanates from your celiac plexus. Of course, since all the chakras interconnect, your third chakra makes sure that all aspects of your body are provided everything they need, from nutrition to fluids.

I like to compare the third chakra to a large wood-fired potbellied stove. If it's kept stoked, the entire house will be warm and happy.

AREAS OF THE BODY MANAGED

Your third chakra governs dozens of significant duties, especially those devoted to digestion. Organs in this area include the liver, gallbladder, spleen, stomach, parts of the esophagus, the small intestine, and the pancreas, which, as I mentioned, has also earned the title of serving as the third chakra's main endocrine gland. Also within its territory are the skin, breath, upper abdomen, diaphragm, middle spine, and parts of the kidneys and adrenals, particularly the adrenal cortex.

Your solar plexus chakra is also intertwined with your enteric nervous system, also called the "gut brain." This aspect of your autonomic nervous system, which relates to stress, is also highly associated with your second or sacral chakra.

Amazingly enough, your body actually has three brains. Your head brain processes thoughts. Your heart brain invites higher awareness. And your gut brain manages your digestive activities, as you might expect, but also most of your feelings, stress reactions, and immune system. That latter is composed of networks of neurons that are buried throughout your digestive tract and linked to your central nervous system. Your enteric nervous system is linked to the heart, head, and most of your body's organs (and the chakras too) through the vagus nerve. This very long cranial nerve is like a winding river that is programmed by your social experience as well as your ancestry, family of origin, life experiences, culture, and more. These codes tell your body how to respond to internal and external stimuli. For instance, while someone else might be just fine if a bee lands on their food, you might freak out; it all depends on this programming. Since at least 90 percent of the signals that run along your vagus nerve pass from your gut brain to your head brain, you can see why the celiac nerve plexus is called the brain of the body.

As I've pointed out, your enteric nervous system incorporates the third as well as the second chakra, which lies in the abdomen and runs some of your small intestine and the entire large intestine. It even flows all the way down to the anus. Much of what determines the health of the overall enteric system starts in the third chakra.

Let's track the stages of your digestion so I can make my point. You eat and drink. Immediately, enzymes in your saliva begin to break down and assist your mouth tissue in absorbing these nutrients. The foodstuff passes downward through the esophagus into your stomach, which continues the digestion process. Depending on the enzymatic interactions between your stomach and gallbladder, liver, and pancreas, the twenty feet of your small intestine will receive material that it will either make use of or that will create health problems, such as the leaky gut syndrome described later in this chapter.

At least 100 million bacteria live in the gastrointestinal tract. This tract is a regular commune, also hosting fungi, parasites, viruses, and even algae. It's important that these microbes dwell symbiotically, as altogether they form a microbiome—a community of microbes that administers metabolic functions and fat distribution and regulates much of your immune system. When this biome is off, which can occur because of physical issues such as eating poorly, using antibiotics, or even undergoing serious stress, the vagus nerve carries negative messages throughout the body. The microbes can't do their job, and you might be struck with any number of problems, from physical to emotional.

ASSOCIATED GLAND:
YOUR PANCREAS

The pancreas is the solar plexus's companion hormone gland. It is an oblong, flat organ located deep in the abdomen and under the left rib cage. One part lies between the stomach and spine and another part lies nestled in the curve of the small intestine. The head of the pancreas is positioned at the third lumbar vertebra.

The pancreas is an important part of the digestive system, playing an essential role in transforming the food we eat into fuel for the body's activities. It basically serves two functions at once. As an endocrine gland, it releases juices—including hormones and enzymes—directly into the bloodstream. It is also an exocrine gland because it releases fluids into ducts. In fact, most of the pancreas functions as an exocrine gland, producing enzymes that aid in digestion. The best-known pancreatic hormone is insulin, which is secreted into the bloodstream to regulate the body's sugar levels.

The link between your third chakra and the pancreas means that problems with the pancreas can cause imbalances in this chakra—and vice versa. One way to assess the relationship between the two is to assess the placement of your pancreas. If it is in the right position, you will feel a pulse at the center of your navel. If you are experiencing headaches, diarrhea, abdominal pain, fatigue, anxiety, or certain other conditions, your pancreas might be displaced.

For instance, a pulse located above and to the left of the navel could indicate the potential for respiratory disorders; to the left, emotional problems; and to the right, energy blockages. Finding the pulse to the right and below the navel indicates digestive disorders.

RELATED PHYSICAL STRESSORS, PROBLEMS, AND ILLNESSES

Third chakra health issues are often related to the digestive system and can involve diseases or conditions in any of the many digestive organs within its purview. The types of problems that show up can include cancers of these organs, diabetes, pancreatitis, kidney and adrenal imbalance, low blood pressure, certain colon diseases, stomach ulcers, certain food disorders (such as anorexia and bulimia), hepatitis, heartburn, hypoglycemia, chronic fatigue, muscular disorders, leaky gut syndrome (caused by bodily toxicity and leakage of toxins into the bloodstream through the walls of the small intestine), and yet another gut problem: small intestinal bacterial overgrowth (SIBO).

Given the modern diet's lack of healthy and clean foods, leaky gut syndrome has become an increasingly common problem. Understanding it depends on knowing that our intestinal lining covers more than 4,000 square feet of surface area.[5] When these linings are working correctly, they are semipermeable to an exact and correct degree. They allow just enough nutrients through the lining into the bloodstream to distribute nourishment. When the food

5   Marcelo Campos, MD, "Leaky Gut: What Is It, and What Does It Mean for You?" Harvard Health Blog, September 12, 2023, https://www.health.harvard.edu/blog/leaky-gut-what-is-it-and-what-does-it-mean-for-you-2017092212451.

isn't digested properly before being received by the small intestine or the walls are too porous, partially digested food, toxins, and microbes will penetrate and enter the body, triggering inflammation and changes in the microbiome.

The liver, tasked with cleaning the blood, is now overwhelmed and can't keep up with its garbage hauling duties; it too becomes challenged. The overall result can be chronic allergies, unhealthy cravings, bloating, fatigue, headaches, confusion, aches and pains, joint pain, difficulty concentrating, as well as more severe illnesses such as autoimmune disorders and depression. Leaky gut is often difficult to treat and usually involves changing the diet at the very least.

SIBO is yet another disorder that is rising in frequency. It occurs when there is an abnormal increase in the bacterial population in the small intestine, especially bacteria that aren't usually found in this area. When poor diet or circumstances such as surgery or disease cause overgrowth of the "wrong" bacteria, the digestive process slows down. The excess bacteria can cause diarrhea, weight loss, bloating, and malnutrition. There are four different types of SIBO, and if you suspect you have it, it's important to see a physician for testing and treatment, and possibly a nutritionist and naturopath to establish a healthy diet.

SUMMARY

Your solar plexus chakra has been known as the center of digestion for hundreds of years. It ought to be, as it is the location of most of your digestive organs and systems. As such, it is central to energizing your life.

Served by the celiac nerve plexus, this chakra plays a dynamic role in creating good health. With the main endocrine gland being the pancreas, it also helps balance your hormones overall. Many of our contemporary diseases and conditions originate in the third chakra because digestion is king and queen of health. Looped into the enteric nervous system and our microbiome, imbalances can include everything from autoimmune challenges to diabetes to malnutrition. Take care of your third chakra's health and it will take care of you.

There is even more fabulous information about your solar plexus chakra to cover. We'll get there in the next chapter through a deep-dive discussion of your psyche.

3

OF THE PSYCHE AND THE SOUL

This chapter is about the psychology of your solar plexus chakra. The word *psychology* is made up of two words: *psyche* or "soul," and *logos* or "study." That means you'll be learning how your soul taps into and operates through your third chakra. Another way to discuss this topic is to use the word *spiritual*. Your third chakra is an ideal vehicle for embodying your spirit, or personal essence.

We've already discovered that your third chakra is the mental center of the chakra zodiac, home to your thoughts. In this chapter I'm going to really delve into this and show you what it means. You'll learn about the various types of thoughts held within the third chakra and, fundamentally, what a thought really is. Also covered will be the types of beliefs addressed by the different organs within this chakra's purview, along with a practice that will assist you in making use of this information.

You'll also find a lot of other interesting perspectives related to this chakra: the age at which it activates and the archetypes associated with it, as well as the different intuitive abilities that are available through it. All in all, this chapter will stoke that gemfire that is your third chakra.

OVERARCHING PSYCHOLOGICAL IMPACT

The psychological center point of the manipura is personal power, which is affected by beliefs and emotions related to the ego. Within this chakra space, you determine your sense of worth and your ability to carry out decisions, but only if you can shift from karma to dharma in decision-making.

Karma is a Hindu concept that we could sum up as "trial by error." Basically, it is the presentation of the life wisdom we must gain to learn about love. Dharma is the education we have already acquired about love and our innate ability to give and receive that powerful virtue. As we learn how to take the higher road of goodness, faith, and charity in our thinking and actions, our road to success becomes filled with wonder and good deeds.

Blockages in the third chakra often manifest as pride, anger, fear, prejudice, or victimization. We can become too critical of others or too sensitive to criticism ourselves. Similarly, we may be easily manipulated emotionally or become emotionally manipulative of others. The point of asserting your third chakra power is in refusing to do any of these. Once we bend our values system, it's always too easy to break it, developing control issues or a false sense of grandeur.

Your personal beliefs can be pictured as thoughts strung together with inner dialogue. They are then cemented in place through your actions. If you overindulge in negativity toward yourself or others, you can fall prey to mental chatter and anxiety. If you ignore your intellect, your mind can become lethargic and you will lack conviction.

The importance of beliefs and of the third chakra was highlighted in my work with an "almost successful" jewelry designer. He had grown up being told that he was too effeminate in comparison to his football-playing older brothers. Every time he found himself about to sign a lucrative design contract, the situation fell apart. We discovered that he was unconsciously sabotaging himself to appear more "masculine." Financial success was perceived as drawing attention to his "too creative" faculties. Once he was able to dismantle the belief that his personality was "less manly" because he was creative, his third chakra became more balanced. The next contract he had on the table went through.

CHAKRA ACTIVATION

Each chakra awakens at a different time during our development from infancy to adulthood. Another way to say this is that each chakra goes "online" at a certain stage. Like a computer, it takes in what is occurring outside the self in relation to its unique bandwidth of physical and subtle energy and draws conclusions about those observations. It then stores these ideas as beliefs, feelings, and even physical sensations. With that programming, the chakra hums along and serves its functions physically, psychologically, and spiritually.

Of course, some of these internal and usually subconscious endpoints are life enhancing, but others are not. Especially in relation to the third chakra, the storage house and determiner of your basic life beliefs and ideologies, it's vital to explore what has been stored inside—sort of like cleaning out a closet filled with clothes and shoes that no longer fit so you can find and use the ones that do.

Your third chakra turns on between the ages of two and a half and four and a half. On the earlier side of this stage, children are learning how to put sentences together. All those big emotions they experience are now getting packaged into expression. Think of the frustration of trying to insert so many encounters and reactions into teeny tiny statements. Hence, the youngster is going to struggle with personal power and boundaries.

A child in this situation needs an adult to assist them in naming and explaining what is going on. That doesn't always happen. A lack of clarity can cause confusion within the third chakra and therefore the child. They require parameters that are neither too rigid nor loose. Too many boundaries will inhibit the expanding child. Too few will be like an invitation to grandiosity.

Increasingly, toward age four and a half, a child develops their mental capabilities. Concepts such as time, shape, color, similarities, and opposites start making sense. And they love to play. If they edge toward being productive during playtime, they might very well enjoy working when they're older. If they are exposed to prejudice and judgment, they will likely adopt those traits when they're older too.

In relation to other chakras, the third chakra activates after the second chakra's light switch has turned on, which follows the turning on of the first chakra, the chakra of physicality and security. From an elemental perspective, the first chakra's earthiness dissolves into the sacral chakra's wateriness. Now we add the fire factor of the solar plexus. The objective is to help a child hold on to the vitality of their second chakra feelings, the core composite of the second chakra, while becoming mentally aware. What we learn during these years can affect us in this endeavor for our entire lives.

PSYCHOLOGICAL FUNCTIONS

The true genius of the solar plexus chakra begins and ends with understanding thoughts.

Our discussion must start with a definition of a thought. Many people believe that thoughts equate with truths, but that is not true. Often defined as opinions, perceptions, or ideas, thoughts are also physical representations or maps. They have shape and weight and depict a subject matter. A thought is not identical to what it symbolizes; rather, in the body, it is an electrochemical formula that starts with a sensory perception. In turn, the sensory impression is converted into a neural signal.[6] That means that a thought cannot be created without a neural event, which makes it physical.

The embodied reality of a thought doesn't make it "true" in a definitive sense. Like all impressions, it is encoded via our perceptions and retrieved in the same way. We have all experienced our memories as not measuring up to what actually occurred in everyday reality. For instance, I used to

6   Ralph Lewis, MD, "What Actually Is a Thought? And How Is Information Physical?" Psychology Today, October 7, 2023, https://www.psychologytoday.com/us/blog/finding-purpose/201902/what-actually-is-thought-and-how-is-information-physical.

recall that the cookie jar my mother had when I was quite small was purple. Years later, she insisted that it was blue. When she died, I found the jar and discovered that she was correct. It was blue.

To best understand and interact with your third chakra, it's imperative to know that the unlimited beliefs that it manages as the brain of the body are neurological, but they are really nothing more or less than perceptions or a lot of maybes. I explain to people that in the energetic realm, thoughts are pinpricks of perceptions. When strung together, they formulate thoughtforms, which could be compared to pearls on a string. When you put a lot of pearl necklaces together, no matter the configuration, you have formulated a paradigm.

Many of us put our faith in paradigms and even live by them. That is often the case when people wholeheartedly adopt the belief system or theology of a religion or type of spirituality, and equally so when they adapt to any "ism," whether it originates in a political party, an ethnicity, or even the core principles that lead to racism, sexism, and genocide. When dealing with your third chakra, if you want to enjoy life in a happy and successful manner, you must examine the core or foundational thoughts underneath the paradigms you operate within to see if they are healthy for you and others—or not.

Ultimately, I'd suggest that most of our thoughts—and I mean the neurological firings determining our ego, personality, and actions—are dysfunctional. There are several basic beliefs that underpin most thoughtforms and paradigms:

» I am bad.

» I am worthless.

» I am undeserving.

» I have no value.

» I am powerless.

» I am unlovable.

What these thoughts have in common is a central ideology, which is this:

Everything and everyone are separate.

The perception of separation leads us to create storylines that make ourselves or others the hero or the villain, but never the twain shall meet. It inevitably leads to judgments, isolation, and the negative beliefs listed above.

The accurate truth, the only one worth building a string of pearls and paradigms upon, is this:

Everything and everyone are connected through love.

When love serves as your central truth, you'll make decisions about your life based on love of self and others. You'll establish boundaries that will assist you in selecting nutritional food, establishing a healthy lifestyle, and working toward success and happiness while rejecting cruelty and hatred. You'll thrive. The following exercise will assist you in doing that.

PRACTICE

ESTABLISH CONNECTION THROUGH YOUR SOLAR PLEXUS

One powerful way to physically balance the manipura is to connect with your solar plexus, front and back, to deliberately exhale all beliefs that are separation based, and inhale and lock in the truth of being connected only to goodness through love.

On a mat or your bed, lie on your stomach and put your hands, one atop the other, under your solar plexus. Breathe long and deep, pressing your hands into your navel while allowing your breathing to massage your abdomen. If you want, you can gently move the lower hand. Imagine that all the thoughts related to the lies of separation are being moved into the air, to be processed by nature. When you feel ready, perhaps after a minute or two, turn over and lie on your back. Simply rest your hands lightly on your solar plexus. Affirm the truth of all love. Let this knowledge stream through your body effortlessly. After a minute, withdraw your hands and relax.

PSYCHOLOGICAL DEFICIENCIES IN AN UNHEALTHY THIRD CHAKRA

Deficiencies in this energy center can include low self-esteem, low self-confidence, contracted energy, and unhappiness with your life situation. Some individuals with an unhealthy solar plexus chakra can act quite borderline, meaning they might throw temper tantrums like a two-year-old to get what they want, thinking that if they scream loudly enough, they might scare people into going along with them. Yet other people are overly frightened of bullies and find themselves giving in all too easily, to their own dismay.

Additional psychological issues might manifest as a victim-or-victor mentality. The victim side of the coin makes you see the world through the lens of being constantly taken advantage of. This can lead to a sense of entitlement. *Since I'm always victimized*, the thinking goes, *the world owes me. I shouldn't have to work for anything.*

The victor side of the coin convinces you that others are simply a means to an end. *If you don't take advantage of them, they'll use you.* Unreliability, aggressiveness, passivity, and a blame/shame attitude are typical factors for the wounded third chakra person.

PSYCHOLOGICAL STRENGTHS
IN THE HEALTHY THIRD CHAKRA

A balanced third chakra results in healthy assertiveness, co-operation, and dynamic energy. Your natural intelligence will shine, and you'll be productive yet take time out to renew your energy when needed. Both your intuition and mind are available to make decisions.

Rather than being judgmental, you'll be characterized as discerning. Without the prejudices that so many people use to arrive at decisions, you'll distinguish yes from no based on what is loving or not. Boundaries are included in that statement, by the way.

With a balanced third chakra, you'll find it relatively easy to draw upon your innate intelligence and be mentally focused when needed. A calendar will be your friend. You'll create and implement protocols, such as keeping goals and appointments, to get where you're aiming. When a problem arises, all will be okay. You won't be overly anal. You will flow around the rock in the river and innovate. All in all, you'll reflect the sunny glow that characterizes this gemfire chakra.

ASSOCIATED ARCHETYPES

An *archetype* is a template or model. There are positive and negative archetypes associated with the third chakra.

The positive archetype of the third chakra is the warrior. This archetype provides a person with an unsurpassable source of power that can be used for achieving worthy causes and making a difference.

The negative archetype is that of servant. All too often, the servant helps others to the exclusion of the self, perhaps secretly hoping for recognition or praise. If used beneficially, however, this approach can enable personal empowerment toward higher service and does not have to remain a negative symbol.

The following short exercise will help you sense the difference between operating as a warrior or a servant.

PRACTICE

TRY ON YOUR THIRD CHAKRA ARCHETYPES

Think of a situation related to your work or your sense of calling. Select one in which you find yourself struggling, maybe wanting to quit, or putting off a challenge.

In a quiet state, picture yourself as a warrior. You can wear the full regalia of a knight or the calm cloak of a Merlin who walks undeterred into danger. Let yourself experience how this vision of yourself influences your perception of the circumstances and how it informs your attitudes and actions toward self and others.

Next, wash away that self-mastery energy and return to the selected situation. Now try on the role of servant. Consider what it feels like to acquiesce, to listen only to others' values or ideas rather than your own.

Activate the red fire element of your third chakra to purify the servile posture from your third chakra. Now decide how you will go forth as a warrior.

THE POWERS OF YOUR THIRD CHAKRA ORGANS

Every third chakra organ supervises a set of beliefs or manages a task for the third chakra. As you read through my understanding of these ideas—a concept I've been teaching for decades—focus on whichever organ might require some extra focus in the moment. Perhaps its energy can assist you in meeting a specific goal or freeing yourself from a negative pattern. You can return to this list anytime you desire.

> **PANCREAS**: Brings joy. Your pancreas delivers energy at a moment's notice and provides insulin to absorb blood sugar for energy or storage. Carbs (sugars) are about empowering action and

thinking. Your pancreas can basically act like a brain to help you decide the "sweetest" path forward—the one deserving of your energy.

LIVER: Meets goals. Besides cleansing and purifying your blood, the liver empowers your movement forward. Help it stay healthy by aiming it where you want to go.

GALLBLADDER: Holds visions. Physically, this organ aids in digesting fats and vitamins. Fats are all about the richness of life, and each vitamin serves its own metaphysical purpose. Help your gallbladder bring to life the wealth of your highest gifts, life visions, and guiding principles.

SPLEEN: Focus. Your very busy spleen fights microbes and transforms nutrients for your overall system and immunity. It also keeps your blood cells healthy. Employ your spleen wisely, as it assists you in fighting off unhealthy ideas and assimilating the ideas that are vital to your life.

STOMACH: Differentiation. With the assistance of enzymes, your stomach breaks down food, fiber, and fluid. It also puts all types of thoughts and ideas together in its cauldron. Let it distinguish between your own and others' mental constructs, and feed it only what you want to make use of.

SMALL INTESTINE: Sorting and processing. All those good nutrients and any unneeded products get separated in this organ. If your philosophies (and diet) are healthy, your small intestine can release what's unhealthy into the large intestine for elimination and send your body what is nourishing.

PERSONALITY PROFILE

If you are strong in the third chakra energy center, you are a thinker. You revel in ideas, facts, information, and concepts, and are driven to organize this information into understandable systems. Because of this, you are a great organizer and administrator.

As the brainiac of all chakra types, you are also terrific at learning and memorizing. So trust what comes into your mind when you must take a test, create a report, or speak intelligently. Give in to your love affair with facts and data and go for it.

Also remember to establish the structures necessary to meet your own or others' goals. Your spiritual destiny will, without a doubt, include working mindfully with knowledge to structure informational processes. Draw on your logic and ability to formulate projects with start and end dates, and try to avoid your natural perfectionism or overly analytic tendencies.

THE INTUITIVE GIFT
OF THE THIRD CHAKRA

Your major intuitive gift is mental empathy. Put in simple terms, you know what others are thinking as well as what motivates and drives them. That can be a challenging gift as sometimes you can confuse what others desire for themselves with what you wish for yourself. Know that while you might be accurate about others' issues and even their thoughts, it doesn't always pay to speak your knowledge out loud.

Another term for your innate psychic strength is claircognizance, or "clear thinking." In the end, what this means is that it's important to trust your gut. That inner knowing in the solar plexus area will give you the yes or no you need. A yes might formulate as a happy feeling deep inside. A no could feel like a dip in energy or a sudden weight falling to the bottom of your stomach. The more you feel into and follow your gut sense, the more often it will work for you. That means you can trust your gut when making decisions.

The following short exercise will help you practice your ability to deeply discern and know.

PRACTICE

MENTAL EMPATHY:
HOW TO INTERPRET A KNOWING

Focus on a decision you need to make. Then place your hands on your solar plexus and breathe into that area.

Come up with one of the choices you're considering and frame it as a question, such as "Would this be a beneficial choice to affirm?" Then let your third chakra provide you with an affirmation, a neutral response, or a definitive no. Here is how you will know what you have received:

» Affirmations will tingle with an exciting feeling in your third chakra. Your bodily energy will rise from your feet to your head and leave you with a "let's go forward" sensation.

» Neutral responses will be blank and flat. There will be little to no extra movement or feelings in your body. If you receive a bland response, come up with another choice and test it.

» Negative reactions will give you a sick feeling in your gut. Your physical energy will feel like it's falling from your head downward, and you'll sense an overall loss of life energy. This is a no.

Keep testing your ideas until you arrive at a clear and rising "go for it."

A FEW OTHER EXTRAORDINARY
SPIRITUAL ABILITIES

Besides mental empathy, several other unusual yet profound spiritual capabilities are linked with a developed third chakra, especially those that have been activated by a rising kundalini.

In Hinduism these are known as *siddhis*. The word embraces a wide variety of powerful and rather miraculous capabilities that occur when we've reached a state of enlightenment, or the higher awareness of love. In accordance with this philosophy, at this juncture the third chakra yogi is granted the *patala siddhi*, the ability to acquire hidden treasures and be freed from disease. Released from the power of fire, the yogi will remain safe even if thrown into the flames. This yogi conquers the ravages of time and can live an extraordinarily long life, discovering cures for illnesses and obtaining a deep understanding of physiology.

May you all obtain equivalent gifts.

SUMMARY

As the focus point of your willpower, manipura is an extraordinary source of cognitive empathy. As you have learned, each associated physical organ carries its own creative and psychological function as well. Understanding these roles will enable you to brainstorm how to assist an organ if it's ever in trouble. And when it comes to third chakra archetypes, being a spiritual warrior instead of a victim or martyr will serve every capacity of your well-being.

I bet you're ready to gain even more practical insights—and put what you're learning into practice. Part 2 will help you do just that.

PART 2

APPLYING THIRD CHAKRA
KNOWLEDGE IN REAL LIFE

. . . . . .

It's time to enjoy the gemstone brilliance and deep intelligence of your third chakra—and yourself.

Each of the following chapters was sculpted for you by a different author. These are subtle energy experts who have personal and professional experience with all the chakras. Their intention is to offer their unique insights about the third chakra so you can become better acquainted with it and enjoy the latent benefits that dwell in your solar plexus center.

You can read these chapters in any order. If you are into spirit allies, you can turn directly to chapter 4. If cooking is a priority, go for the recipes in chapter 13.

Make way for the depth of knowledge, inspiration, and practices presented by the featured authors in part 2, and get ready to be empowered by the sunshine of your third chakra.

YOU'LL BE USING INTENTION

Here are the keys to benefiting from the practices your expert companions offer in part 2: comprehending the power of setting an intention and knowing how to create one.

The term "intention" is equivalent to a desire—but so much more. When you establish an intention and infuse it with your heart and soul, you invite a change in your everyday world. The subtle energy of an intention becomes activated and compelled to rearrange physical reality, and thus does a dream come true.

You could say that the entire world is a materialization of intention—a mixture of prayers, hopes, and dreams made manifest. If you want to alter what is appearing in the universe or in your own mini ecosystem, you can shape an intention and then go about making it real.

The simplest way to formulate an intention is to create a statement of desire. There are three parts to this action. First, you focus on a desire or need and compose a one-sentence statement based on it. That sentence should have at least a noun (subject) and then a verb (action), and end with the desire expressed in present time. Use words that are positive and optimistic, such as "I am enjoying my job as a well-paid accountant."

Now add emotion to your intention. Let yourself feel as if it has already occurred. *Yes.* You have that amazing job—or whatever you are attracting—and are grateful for it. In fact, you are assuming that it exists, and you could just plain jump for joy because you have achieved it. Emotions are "energy in motion" and serve to bring the world to your fingertips and invite you to appropriate action.

The third step is to reiterate your manifesting decision. Think about it daily. Sing it as a chorus while you're washing your hands. Roll the words around in your head and remind yourself of how gleeful you are that it has come true.

I'd love to have you practice creating an intention right now, just to try it out. You can also use this exercise with any of the chapters in part 2.

PRACTICE

SETTING A THIRD CHAKRA INTENTION

Dwell on a desire relating to your third chakra: a job, work success, sense of personal power, self-confidence, intellectual understanding—you get it. Now package your aspiration into an inspirational statement; for example, if you want to start your own business, you could say something like this:

*I am thriving in my new business
as a self-confident entrepreneur.*

Now walk around with that intention as your mantra. Color it yellow, write it on your bathroom mirror, dress for the success you're going to have. You can always set a new intention if you think follow-up is necessary.

And just like that, you are landing your future in the here and now.

4

SPIRIT ALLIES

MARGARET ANN LEMBO

You have an entourage of energetic assistants helping you in all aspects of life. Mind-to-mind and heart-to-heart communication with spirit allies uses thoughts, feelings, and visualization. It's called telepathy. It's the most direct way to tap into the invisible allies that are everywhere in many forms.

Spirit allies are available to everyone. Ask for guidance and assistance from these energetic allies, and relax into knowing you are not alone.

Let's get familiar with the energies of these invisible helpers so you can be discerning and invite only those working for your highest good. You can feel the essence of these helpers, available through your solar plexus chakra, on a vibrational level.

Consider spirit allies in many forms: angels and archangels; the plant spirits or devic forces of essential oils; animal allies; and gemstone guardians (refer to my section about working with crystals and gemstones in chapter 10).

ANGELS, ANIMAL ALLIES, AND DEVIC FORCES

When I was a child, I realized that plants have consciousness. Energy and vibration are present in every plant and flower and all aspects of nature. My interest in communication with nature, plants, and animals started in the garden with my mother.

The seen and unseen are both real worlds; the beings and energies of both help guide and light our path. Spirit allies influence us, and we receive guidance from all of nature. Tune in to your heart and your mind, and communication from nature will flow.

The solar plexus chakra is the center for your ability to take in, absorb, and integrate life. The solar plexus manages the vibration of experiencing and digesting all that you see and experience around you. Work with the spirit allies profiled below to bring mental clarity, joy, self-confidence, and the ability to integrate life experiences. These are also the allies to help improve self-esteem and your ability to see life from a greater perspective. Call on these spirit allies to maintain your ability to establish boundaries with ease and grace whenever necessary.

ANGELS AND ARCHANGELS

Angels and archangels—beings of light, color, and vibration—do not have a gender. For definition, angels are a broad term for these messengers of the Divine, while archangels are a specific rank of angel that is entrusted to specific holy and practical tasks. Your angelic helpers act and react based on your thoughts, prayers, and petitions for assistance. Give them permission to inspire you with guidance and wisdom. First I'll introduce you to angels and then to a mighty archangel.

Angel of Change

The solar plexus chakra is the chakra of self-esteem and the courage to live to your full potential. The digestion of food and the digestion of life are essential aspects of the energy here and how you integrate life. With this angel on your team, you can recognize that life flows in circles and all cycles shift and change. Let this angel help you focus on how you want your reality to manifest in alignment with the changes that are occurring.

The Angel of Change is always helping you shift and flow with change because, after all, the only constant in life is change. The Angel of Change supports you so that you can stop worrying and have the faith and courage you need to navigate life's twists and turns.

Angels need permission to help you, so ask the Angel of Change to help you relax and flow with the ever-turning cycles that create change. Petition this angel to help you easily adapt and make the necessary adjustments so that life is happy and fulfilling.

> **AFFIRMATIONS:** It is easy for me to make the changes I need to in order to transform my life. Challenging situations are opportunities to create something better for me and those around me. I modify my behavior to bring more joy into my life. Change is good.

Angel of Fun and Play

Call on the Angel of Fun and Play when you need extra help to activate your core of happiness and playfulness. Think about what would make you happy today. Think about what activity would make you feel like you are having fun.

Call on the Angel of Fun and Play when you realize you've been too serious and might be working too hard. This angel encourages you to pause and remember how to enjoy life more fully. When you were a child, playing was an essential part of developing your brain, body, and social skills. Play is also a key part of maintaining a healthy body, mind, and spirit as an adult. Having fun is a perfect tool to relieve toxic stress and support emotional resilience.

Ask for guidance, and let this angel help you take much-needed time to relax and play. Ask for inspiration to find creative ways to relax and use your imagination, stimulate your mind, carve out leisure time, and activate your body to engage in fun, rejuvenating play the way you did as a child.

AFFIRMATIONS: Joy and happiness are a
normal part of my day. Play, work, rest,
exercise, and laughter balance me. I am
grateful for all that is good in my life.

Angel of Inner Strength and Setting Boundaries

Self-confidence and courage are essential components within the energy of the solar plexus chakra. Call on this angel when you need to have fortitude and resolve to make positive choices. This is the angel to petition when you need to call on your core strength and courage to withstand adversity. Within this band of energy, this angel will inspire and support your efforts to establish limits with people who demonstrate inappropriate behavior. The Angel of Inner Strength and Setting Boundaries helps you discern when to establish a boundary.

Remember that your true nature is love and that you choose how you respond to other people. Instead of reacting to unpleasant people, take a moment to breathe and say a little prayer for them and yourself. As you send off a request for assistance from this angel, envision that confidence and inner strength are well established, to the core of your being. Have courage, speak up for yourself with ease and grace, and step into your personal power with awareness.

> **AFFIRMATIONS:** I am courageous. I am able to set boundaries when necessary. I am self-confident. The past provides me with the experience necessary to improve my self-esteem.

Guardian Angel

Your guardian angel is the angel assigned to you at birth for this lifetime. Your guardian angel helps you feel guided and safe as you navigate the changing landscape of your life. Call on this angel for anything and everything. Petition your guardian angel when you need help with any situation. Invite your angel to light your path in alignment with your highest and best good.

You always have this invisible helper nearby, just waiting to serve you. All you need to do is ask. Remember to use specific requests when asking for this angel's assistance. Just think these thoughts with your guardian angel in mind, and help will be on the way. Use the various insights and practices throughout this book as inspiration for wording your request. Use your imagination, and ask this angel to help you stand in your personal power, establish healthy boundaries, recognize your magnificence, and live your life with self-confidence. You can truly stand in your brilliance, do or achieve anything you put your attention to, and become anyone you want to be.

> **AFFIRMATIONS:** I have an entourage of angels
> that guide me. I manage situations that
> arise. I step into my personal power. I am
> blessed with supportive friends and family.

Archangel Michael

Call on Archangel Michael to help you believe in yourself. Michael can remind you that your inner strength and high self-esteem provide a service to your family, your community, and the world. Have the courage to truly speak and act from your heart. Follow your heart in all you do. Recognize the good and acknowledge it. Have the self-confidence and self-esteem needed to make a difference.

Archangel Michael is dedicated to protecting you. He helps remove fears and phobias that might distract you from your intentions. Call on Archangel Michael to bring feelings of comfort and safety your way. Archangel Michael is often portrayed wearing silver armor and carrying a round shield and a sword to ward off malevolent situations, negative people, and inner and outer demons. Archangel Michael can help you cut the cords of attachment to negative people, places, and situations that no longer support your highest good.

> **AFFIRMATIONS:** I radiate light. I am passionate and live life to the fullest. I am blessed to have respectful friends, family, and colleagues who respect me and my person.

ANIMAL ALLIES

The connectedness of everything on our planet—from rocks and crystals to plants and animals—links messages and lessons from the animal kingdom to your consciousness for personal awareness and growth. Here are a few animal allies who will bring you messages and realizations on your spiritual journey.

Armadillo

Call on the energy of Armadillo when you are attempting to set boundaries and stand up for yourself. With Armadillo as an ally, you are shielded from negativity as you look below the surface to know the truth. Whenever you want to avoid people in certain places or situations, call on the energy of Armadillo to support you. Make it your intention to establish a clear energetic vibration that keeps others from invading your energy with hurtful words or bad intentions.

> **AFFIRMATIONS:** I set boundaries gently
> and with grace. I am selective about the
> people who are part of my inner circle. I
> embrace being powerful and confident.

Lion

When Lion steps into your life, learn to be a team player. If you have a great idea that seems larger than life, find the courage to take it on. Your willingness to do something big might be the foundation for others to have the revenue to feed themselves and their family. Invite others to support your big vision; they can also benefit.

> **AFFIRMATIONS:** I am self-assured. I show my true self
> in all situations. I have integrity. I allow others to
> see my brilliance as I exude self-assurance.

Ram

Ram is an ally for you when you need extra strength and endurance to overcome problems or situations that require you to rise above the ordinary and see a challenge through to a successful resolution. Use this energy to help enhance endurance, courage, good health, and strong physical structure. Ram's vibe is aligned with the solar plexus's quality that helps you take the higher road, even when the higher road requires strength and bravery. Ram's message encourages you to act, do it now, be a leader, and support others when it is their turn to lead the way.

> **AFFIRMATIONS:** I am energetic. I happily share my time. I am vivacious and resilient. I finish what I set out to do. I am unwavering.

AROMATHERAPEUTIC ALLIES

Aromatherapy is the use of essential oils derived from plants' aromatic parts—in the form of simple oils, mists, incenses, or sprays that heal physical, mental, and emotional complaints and improve your overall well-being. Establishing intention and accessing the unlimited potential provided by your imagination are important components of working with aromatherapy to bring balance to your chakras. Here are a few that are beneficial for improving the solar plexus energy center.

Anise Seed Essential Oil

Anise seed is your ally when you are overwhelmed and finding it difficult to integrate everything that is going on in your life. The solar plexus is the energy center for digestion, including how you digest life and food. Inhale this essential oil to balance the absorption of sugar and stimulate your digestive system toward balance. Use anise seed in a synergistic blend intended for protection or to support high levels of self-esteem and joy.

AFFIRMATIONS: I have a healthy digestion. I am present in each moment and have situational awareness. I am focused and alert. I am joyful and enthusiastic.

FOR YOUR SAFETY: Use anise seed sparingly or occasionally as overuse can be carcinogenic. It is a possible skin irritant. Use with caution if on diabetes medication as it affects blood sugar levels. Avoid use in cases of endometriosis and estrogen-dependent cancers. Do not use if pregnant or nursing.

Bergamot Essential Oil

Bergamot is beneficial physically at the solar plexus chakra in relation to its ability to activate digestive enzymes and bile. The clean, fresh aroma of bergamot is a palate cleanser to the mind. Use it to clear away fogginess and bring focus and clarity. This uplifting oil aids in thinking good thoughts about yourself and increases awareness of all your positive qualities.

AFFIRMATIONS: Focus and clarity are natural to me. Joy and courage are natural to me. My digestive system is healthy. I integrate all that is going on.

FOR YOUR SAFETY: This oil is phototoxic (and potentially photocarcinogenic); therefore, avoid exposure to direct sunlight when using topically. Do not use old or oxidized bergamot. Avoid use in cases of kidney disease. Do not use if pregnant or nursing.

Cinnamon Essential Oil

Cinnamon raises your confidence and self-esteem. It helps free the energy we call "blocks," allowing you to move beyond the perception that something is standing in the way of your goals, desires, or the completion of creative projects. Inhale this essential oil while you repeat the affirmations to shine your light and be all that you can be.

AFFIRMATIONS: My imagination helps me to be a success! I am brave. I easily manifest what I need and want. I have great ideas. I enjoy life and have a passion for living.

FOR YOUR SAFETY: Do not use topically; use only for aromatherapy. Do not use if pregnant or nursing.

Lemon Essential Oil

Lemon essential oil helps when you are recovering from the blues. Use lemon essential oil in synergistic blends to help raise your spirits. This golden-yellow vibration assists you in garnering self-confidence when you are on a quest to improve your self-esteem.

> **AFFIRMATIONS:** I twinkle with light, and the light
> I radiate helps others find joy. I am grateful
> for who I am and what I have accomplished
> in my life. I am poised and brave.

> **FOR YOUR SAFETY:** This oil is phototoxic;
> therefore, avoid exposure to direct
> sunlight when using topically.

SUMMARY

Spirit allies are ready to assist you with any of your third chakra concerns. You learned about many forms of these brilliant beings in this chapter: angels and archangels, plant spirits and devic forces of essential oils, and animal allies; gemstone allies will be covered in chapter 10. Each can be tapped with intention to facilitate high-level awarenesses for healing and manifesting. Enjoy the affirmations in this chapter—and the existence of these spirit helpers in your life.

5

YOGA POSES

AMANDA HUGGINS

Of the lower three chakras, the solar plexus is my personal favorite to work with. Located just a few inches above the belly button, this chakra is where we derive our confidence and sense of personal power. In yoga, this energy center is physically activated in almost all poses as the abdomen is the locus for both movement and stability. When we combine energetic and physical aspects of the gemfire chakra in yoga, it manifests as a beautiful expression of inner and outer strength.

I've always found it fascinating that this energy center, one that is deeply connected to confidence and expansion, is in the belly—a part of the body that Western society has demanded we keep small. Through the media, we've been conditioned to suck in our bellies: *Make it flatter. Tighter. Smaller. Heck, make it invisible altogether.* As we've absorbed this subconscious programming, we've taken on the fear of taking up space, both literally and metaphorically.

Yoga radically counteracts the external demand to self-minimize, instead inviting you to expand physically, mentally, and energetically. Your yoga practice wants you to breathe deeply and expansively into the belly. It encourages you to take up space. Most importantly, it affirms your divine birthright, inviting you to know *I am in my power*.

ACTIVATING THE SOLAR PLEXUS THROUGH YOGIC BREATHWORK

The solar plexus can be physically activated. We use the abdominals in almost all poses, but the foundation for engaging this energy center is through the breath.

Kapalabhati pranayama—also known as Skull Shining Breath or Breath of Fire—is an active form of yogic breathwork that connects you to the solar plexus and circulates energy throughout the body. It's a wonderful way to build heat before engaging in *asanas* (body poses). It is also a great tool as a stand-alone practice for releasing excess energy or clearing solar plexus blockages.

PRACTICE

KAPALABHATI BREATHING

DISCLAIMER: It is best to practice Breath of Fire, another name for this style of breathing, on an empty stomach (which you'll soon understand after practicing on your own). Also note this practice is not recommended for those who may be pregnant or actively menstruating.

Preparation

If you're new to kapalabhati pranayama, I suggest practicing this technique in front of a floor-length mirror, if possible. Doing so allows you to see how you're physically activating the abdominals.

To prepare, sit in whatever way is comfortable for you. You can use a mat, the floor, a chair, or any other support.

I like to move the spine around a bit first, circling or undulating the upper body to create space before coming to stillness. From stillness, connect with your solar plexus by bringing your focus to the abdominal space. Fully release any sucking in and let the belly go as you take three to five cycles of deep breathing.

As you breathe, observe how this energy center feels. If you're feeling spacious and powerful, you may choose to set an intention to increase that sense of empowerment. If you're feeling blocked, drawn in, or otherwise minimized, you may set an intention to release that energy through the breath.

The Practice

Kapalabhati breathing is focused on short, vigorous exhalations through the nose.

Start with a full inhale. On the exhale, forcefully expel the breath through the nostrils while simultaneously drawing the abdomen in toward the spine. The exhales should be audible.

The inhales should feel passive, or automatic, as you fully let the belly release and expand outward. Immediately expel the air again through the nose by drawing the navel inward. Repeat this breath pattern at a vigorous pace (about one exhale per second) for ten to twenty cycles to start. Rest for one minute in stillness, bringing your attention (and intention) to the energy in your solar plexus. Repeat the entire process twice more.

If you're not sure you're doing it right, YouTube is a great resource. Search for "kapalabhati pranayama tutorial," "skull shining breath how-to," or "breath of fire for beginners." You'll quickly find loads of great videos that will demonstrate the abdominal activation and the sound of the breath.

Closing the Practice

After you feel complete, take a final cycle of deep yogic breathing before returning to breathing normally. Before rising, set a power-filled mantra for yourself.

GENERATING PHYSICAL AND EMOTIONAL POWER THROUGH ASANAS

There is a beautiful feedback loop that occurs when you work with your third chakra through yoga. As you stand (literally) in your physical power in each pose, you'll begin generating and circulating the nonphysical essence of power (the feeling and knowing of your power on an emotional level) throughout your body.

For example, you may experience a swell of positive energy and confidence or even feel proud of yourself as you hold yourself powerfully in a pose. In a different pose, you might find yourself needing to tap into that power-filled feeling again to restore confidence and stability when you're feeling shaky or insecure. You're stoking your inner fire and allowing that energy to circulate throughout the physical body and your entire energetic field.

Yoga is abundant in poses—both restorative and active— that offer fantastic activations of the solar plexus.

There are a few key poses that directly target this energy center by working the abdominal space. Take *bhujangasana*, or cobra pose, for example. In cobra, your belly is flush to the ground, which provides a physical feedback point and allows you to really feel the engagement of your abdominal muscles (and solar plexus).

Twists are also a fantastic option for working this energy center. Twisting postures require deep, expansive breathing to create space in the body and allow you to physically wring out stuck energy. I love to energetically check in when I'm in a twist and ask myself: "What can I let go of in this moment to create more room for where I'm going?" Sometimes that question is just about the physical aspect (let go of that resistance in the abs and let that twist happen), while at other times the energy of that question goes much deeper. In either case, dialoguing with the solar plexus in twists can be a powerful way to create space.

PRACTICE

FULL YOGA FLOW TO ACTIVATE THE THIRD CHAKRA

Before diving into the suggested yoga flow, set your intention for your practice. Here are some solar plexus intentions to serve as inspiration. Feel free to pick and choose what works for you. Make the intentions your own.

» I derive my confidence and
sense of self from within.

» I am deeply trusting of my body,
my heart, and my spirit.

» I am worthy and inherently powerful.

» I am releasing energies of shame,
criticism, and unworthiness today.

» I am creating space for empowered
transformation.

» I am powerful in my own unique way.

Begin by standing in mountain pose, with one or both
hands resting on your solar plexus. Take five deep breaths
here as you connect to your intention and energy center.

» warm up the body with five half sun salutations

A "half salutation" is just a traditional sun salutation.
Stand at the front of your mat and inhale as you lift both
arms overhead. Dive forward with a flat back and fold in
toward yourself. Inhale and lift your spine halfway. Exhale
and fold back in toward yourself. Inhale and rise back up to
standing. Repeat four more times.

On the fifth and final round, rather than rising back to
a standing position, plant your hands on the mat and walk
your body into a plank position.

» hold plank position for five cycles of breath

A plank position involves holding the trunk of your body in a straight line off the ground with your elbows directly under your shoulders and your palms flat on the floor, just like you are doing a push-up. Your feet are about hip-width apart in that same push-up position.

Draw attention to your abdominal muscles and channel that physical power when you begin to tremble. After the last round of breath, lower yourself flat to the ground.

» move into bhujangasana (cobra pose)

Lie face down on your mat with your feet a few inches apart. Take a few deep breaths. Place your hands under your shoulders with your fingers pointing toward the front of the mat and your elbows out to the sides. Press the tops of your feet, thighs, and pubic bone into the mat and spread your toes. Inhale as you gently lift your head and upper chest off the mat, keeping your lower ribs on the mat. Straighten your arms as far as is comfortable and draw your shoulders back and your chest forward, looking upward.

There should be almost no weight on your hands. You should not be using a tremendous amount of arm strength here; the lift comes from engaging your abdominal and back muscles.

Exhale and release your forehead to the mat. Repeat three to five more times. With each repetition, aim to create easeful engagement and lengthening of the abdominal muscles. Let the pose emerge from the solar plexus. On your last exhale, you will go into downward-facing dog.

» downward-facing dog, knee to nose

Start in the table position on all fours, hands and knees. Spread your palms wide and stack your shoulders over your wrists. Your knees are about hip-width apart and your toes are curled under. Walk your palms out to just in front of your shoulders, making sure they are flat. Ground in your palms and raise your knees off your mat while shifting your belly toward your thighs. Lift your hips up high and keep your legs straight and your toes pointed forward.

Take a big, expansive breath into the belly and lift your right leg up to the sky. Exhale and bring the right knee to the nose. Hold here for three to five seconds ("Mississippi" style counting). Then plant the right foot in between your hands and find a low lunge.

» low lunge

With your right foot between your hands, settle the left knee down onto the mat. As you inhale, lift torso and arms to the sky. Stay for three to five cycles of breath. You may find yourself wobbly here; that's okay. Use every wobble as a sign you need to root down more. Steady the breath, and release.

> » rise to a high lunge

Lift your hands and torso to the sky. Take a generous bend in the front (right) knee. You should be on the ball of your back (left) foot, with a slight bend in the back knee to protect your lower back. Take three deep, power-filled breaths here. Move into a high lunge twist.

> » high lunge twist

Bring both hands to prayer position in front of the heart. Inhale. Exhale and twist to the right, hooking your left elbow on the right knee. If this is not accessible in your body, simply twist to your degree of comfort, without introducing pain in the body. Breathe, feel, and clear that energy. This is a wonderful place to release energetic blocks. Inhale to find length in the body, and exhale to twist more deeply. Let those inhales be spacious. Take up space, even as you twist. Stay here for three to five cycles of breath. Release the pose and return to downward-facing dog.

> » repeat that sequence of downward-facing dog, knee to nose, low lunge, high lunge, and high lunge twist on the left side

If you'd like to continue building heat and power in the body, you may repeat the entire series (right and left sides) three more times.

» child's pose

Ah, sweet release.

Find child's pose by kneeling on the floor and resting your seat atop your heels. Let the torso drape forward over the knees and extend your hands toward the front of the mat. The knees can be opened or closed; choose the position that feels most comfortable. This is your space to cool down and check in with your energy center. Observe, feel, notice. Allow this to be a noncritical, restful, and empowering moment of pause. Stay here for five to eight breaths and then move on.

» boat pose

Come to a seat on the floor with your legs straight out in front of you. Place both hands on the floor near your hips. Lift through your sternum and lean back slightly as you bring both knees to a 45-degree angle. Make sure your back doesn't round here. If it does, bend the knees more or use your hands behind the thighs for balance. If you're feeling spacious here, you can also extend the legs straight. This is where you're working those abdominal muscles. Breathe deeply into the belly as you close your eyes and tune in to your strength. Stay here for three breaths, then release. Repeat twice more.

» spinal twists

Finally, a restorative pose.

Lie on your back and draw both knees into the chest, as if you're giving yourself a hug. It might feel nice to rock from side to side and massage the spine here. After a few rocks from side to side, allow the knees to drop over to one side. Bring the arms into a T-shape straight out from your shoulders, and gently shift your gaze to the direction opposite your knees. Be fully here. Let your belly get soft as you take deep, restorative breaths and bask in the physical heat you've generated. Stay here for five to eight breaths. Switch sides.

» *savasana* (corpse pose): final resting pose

Close this practice by lying on the floor with your palms facing up. Or you may choose to rest both palms on the belly to connect with your third chakra energy. Allow the earth beneath you to support the entirety of your body weight. Let the breath's natural rhythm arise. You may choose to envision the color yellow enveloping your body as you softly breathe and release. Stay here for as long as you'd like.

SUMMARY

As you practice generating power on the mat—or any-where you do yoga—you will naturally begin to feel energy moving in your solar plexus. But don't forget that power, confidence, and expansion have always lived within you. Keep taking up space and letting your light shine.

6

BODY WISDOM

LINDSAY FAUNTLEROY

My personal healing crisis introduced me to the healing modalities that became the heart of my integrative practice: flower essence therapy, yoga, herbalism, and acupuncture. These practices draw on an indigenous and African diasporic worldview that perceives mind, body, spirit, nature, and the cosmos as an interconnected whole. These healing traditions have been passed down since ancient times to answer the questions that we explore today through modern psychology, biomedicine, and spirituality: Who are we? How are we? And why are we?

No matter our ethnicity or lineage, we are all descended from ancestors who viewed nature as a mirror, an ally, and a sentient source of intelligence and wisdom. For more information on that topic, I highly recommend Edward Bruce Bynum's book *Our African Unconscious: The Black Origins of Mysticism and Psychology*.

This chapter introduces practices to help you embody nature's wisdom as you heal your third chakra.

ACUPRESSURE: ENERGETIC POWER PORTALS

Imagine that your manipura is a place called Sun City: a large metropolis pulsing with vibrant energy. The meridians utilized in acupressure are the energetic highways that cross through Sun City, each bringing resources (chi, life force, or prana) to the major tourist attractions on its route. These attractions are the organs and glands of Sun City: the stomach, spleen, pancreas, adrenals, gallbladder, and liver.

When traffic is flowing through the meridians, we experience good health and the positive soul qualities of the manipura: vitality, healthy ego, confidence, discrimination in our ideas, and the ability to translate thoughts into action. When there's a roadblock in one of the meridians, it puts stress on the other highways that flow through Sun City. We experience this as the physical complaints that were discussed in chapter 2. We also experience the imbalanced soul qualities of the solar plexus: self-doubt, weak willpower, manipulation of others, or inflated ego. We can use acupressure points to clear these energetic traffic jams and regulate the chi flowing in and out of our brilliant Sun City.

ACUPRESSURE FOR
DYNAMIC ENERGY PORTALS

You can use all the following acupressure points to activate the third chakra. You'll begin working with each in the same way.

Rest your fingertips lightly on each dynamic energy portal. Look for a subtle sense of warmth or radiance. Use a light touch; your skin should not indent under your fingertips. You can also use vibrational remedies such as tuning forks, essential oils, flower essences, and gemstones on these points. See chapters 9 and 10 for vibrational remedies that resonate with the third chakra.

Stomach 25: Tianshu (Heaven's Pivot)

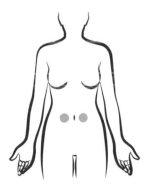

LOCATION: *Alongside the navel, two finger-widths away from the midline*

The stomach and spleen meridians support the earth element in acupuncture theory and are two of the most important highways for Sun City. When they are out of balance, we experience symptoms such as digestive issues, weight gain, weak muscles, emotional eating, blood disorders, head fogginess, fatigue (especially after eating), mucus or phlegm, and sugar cravings. These two channels also regulate the pancreas, spleen, and other organs associated with digestion. Tianshu supports the digestion of not just food but also information, emotions, and experiences.

Liver 3: Taichong (Supreme Surging)

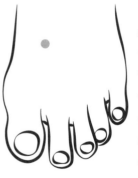

LOCATION: *Top of the foot, in the space between the metatarsal bones of your big toe and second toe*

The liver meridian and its partner, the gallbladder meridian, treat conditions of their namesakes. They are also used to boost the confidence, clarity, and vision that are required for decisive action. Taichong is an adaptogenic source point for the wood element in acupuncture theory. It can be stimulated to either increase your sense of agency and personal power or calm the nervous system when you're feeling overwhelmed with anger or aggression.

Bladder 23: Shenshu (Vital Transfer to the Kidneys)

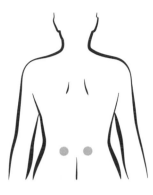

LOCATION: *Lower back, just atop the adrenal glands*

Shenshu connects us to our deepest reserves of energy and vitality. It is used when we are experiencing deep fatigue or burnout and need to jump-start manipura's engine. Rub your hands together to create a sense of warmth and vitality between your palms. Gently rest your hands on your lower back just above your kidneys, radiating warmth to shenshu. You can also use a heating pad or hot water bottle to revitalize this power portal.

PRACTICE

LISTEN TO YOUR BODY
VIA YOUR INNER SUN

This practice involves listening to your body's wisdom by paying attention to the sensations of expansion, contraction, or movement in your body when you contemplate a situation for which you are seeking insight. While our minds tend to validate what we want to believe, our bodies do not lie.

Rest your hands on your belly at your solar plexus. Begin by taking several deep breaths to settle into meditative contemplation and call to mind a question, as if using your body as an oracle. For example, you might ask:

» How is my third chakra shining in this situation?

» What kind of solar expression do I need for success in this endeavor?

Wait patiently for a solar image representing your manipura to emerge. Here are a few suggested interpretations; be sure to check in with your gut knowing for an internal sense of resonance.

Rising Sun

In the sunrise phase, you are growing in confidence, agency, and your ability to be present unapologetically. The warm, red-orange glow rising in the east allows you to see your environment more clearly. A rising sun means you are building your vitality or beginning to see the full dynamics of the situation.

High Noon Sun

A bright golden-yellow high noon sun in your mind's eye may indicate that your third chakra is fully charged with vitality. You are expressing yourself fully and uncompromisingly as you shine your light or you may be feeling a longing to do so.

Setting Sun

A setting sun is retreating from dominance and descending into a period of rest and renewal. If the sun in your solar plexus is setting, reflect on whether the circumstance you inquired about is an invitation to turn down your intensity or welcome the light of fellow stars. You may also be approaching the completion of a cycle.

Eclipsed or Clouded Sun

If the sun that appears in your inner imagery is an eclipsed sun or a sun on a cloudy day, this may indicate a situation where your light is being blocked or unappreciated. Decide if others are undervaluing you or underestimating what you offer or if you are having a hard time acknowledging your own sunshine.

Take a moment to reflect in your journal about the type of sun your gemfire chakra is manifesting.

PRACTICE

TAKE A LION'S BREATH

The image of the lion appears in many myths across cultures as a symbol of courage, bravery, and ferocity. In the tarot, the lion pictured on the Strength card symbolizes our primal instincts and vitality. The lion's association with the zodiac sign Leo connects this archetypal animal ally to our exploration of our identity, personal expression, and ego. Sketch, paint, or collect pictures of lions as you tune in to your solar plexus. Imagine a lion's mane as the radiant rays of the sun and a fiery roar resounding from your gut as you take up space.

Open your mouth wide and stick your tongue out as far as you can, allowing it to reach toward your chin. Inhale through your nose, and then breathe out while making the "ha" sound. Imagine that the sound starts in your belly, rises through your throat, and flows out into the world. It's okay to make some noise—in this breath and in life. Relax and return to your normal breath before repeating the lion's breath four to six times.

PRACTICE

FELLOWSHIP WITH THE
DANDELION AND SUNFLOWER

The following exercise is an adaptation of Carl Jung's active imagination process and is a powerful practice to deepen your relationship with nature's intelligence. Begin by choosing a way to record this meditation, for which you will be flowing between conscious asking and intuitive, imaginative listening. Use a pen of one color for your questions and another color for what you "hear" in response.

Find an image of a dandelion or sunflower. If you can do this exercise with the actual flower, even better. You can see the descriptions of the flowers following this process, and additional suggestions for how to interact with each flower are included in these depictions.

With heartfelt attention, silently invite the soul of the flower to converse with you. Introduce yourself and share why you feel drawn to this flower. Though this dialogue is imaginal, try to embrace it as our ancestors would: as an intuitive interaction with a sentient, conscious being.

Some great questions to get the "conversation" started include:

» What can you teach me?

» Why did you capture my attention?

» What insight can you offer?

Allow compassion and love for yourself and nature to fill your dialogue. Pay attention to what emerges, and resist the urge to overthink or rationalize what you hear in response to your questions. If you find yourself wondering if you are making this up, you are doing it right. Drawing, sketching, or painting the flower is another creative way to tune in to the flower's intelligence without leaving a meditative state of awareness. When it is time to close, thank the flower for its time and wisdom. Then, to honor your reciprocal relationship with nature, recycle, compost, garden, or pick up trash from the ground.

Dandelion

Dandelion is a bright golden flower that resembles a radiant sun. This flower's name was derived from the French phrase meaning "lion's teeth." It's not surprising that dandelion grows abundantly in New York City, a place that resonates strongly with the pulse of the solar plexus. Like the chakra, it has so much light, activity, and vitality. Unfortunately, it also has a lot of selfishness, greed, and manipulation, all expressions of a solar plexus that is out of balance.

When our third chakra is hyper-activated, we push too hard, relying on our personal willpower. We deplete our vital resources while accumulating tension and toxicity in our cells. Dandelion supports these physical, emotional, mental, and spiritual imbalances of the solar plexus. Dandelion leaves can be eaten raw in a salad, and dandelion is a well-known herbal medicine used for liver detoxification. When used topically, dandelion essential oil in a carrier oil or bath can release tension from muscles that are achy, stiff, or overworked by a driven manipura energy center. As a flower essence, dandelion teaches us how to release tension that our body is holding. As you converse with the dandelion, experience what it can teach you about how you manage your stress.

Sunflower

When used as a food, oil, or herbal tincture, sunflower regulates our relationship with internal and external fire. Sunflower oil is great for cooking because it can reach high temperatures without breaking down into chemicals that are harmful for the body. Sunflower seeds are not only a delicious snack but they also provide nutrients such as vitamin E, flavonoids, and other plant compounds that can reduce inflammation. In traditional herbal medicine, sunflower leaves were boiled into teas to reduce fever.

In flower essence therapy, the sunflower harmonizes the personal forces of the ego and the solar principle of the self.

This aspect of the self is responsible for integrating our experiences into an essential wholeness, just as the many planets in our solar system are unified by the sun. Sunflower helps us reconnect to our radiant gemfire light when we don't realize our own value, boundaries, or agency. Embrace what sunflower teaches you about your powerful, radiant ego forces.

PRACTICE

HAKINI MUDRA VARIATION FOR SUNFLOWERS

Like humans, sunflowers have an internal circadian rhythm. A young blossom begins each day facing the east and turns its flower face to track the sun throughout the day. At sunset, sunflowers sink their heads and return to face the east in eager anticipation of the next day's sunrise. This mudra variation embodies the wisdom of the sunflower as it pushes up toward the sun, reaching intuitively and unapologetically for light.

See the opposite page for an example of this sunshiny mudra.

Bring your hands to the height of your solar plexus, palms facing each other. Draw your fingertips together until they touch, spread wide like a radiant sunflower. Bring your thumbs to rest gently on your solar plexus.

Take a deep inhalation, filling your belly with vibrant life force. As you exhale, with fingers still touching, extend your arms directly in front of you, pointing with clear direction toward the path you choose to follow. On your next inhale, raise your arms until they are directly overhead, like a sunflower facing the high noon sun. On the next exhale, separate your hands and extend your arms in a wide circle, embodying the radiant glow of the sun. Return to the Hakini Mudra as you complete the circle by again bringing your fingertips to touch and your thumbs to your solar plexus. Repeat this cycle for several breaths.

THE HAKINI MUDRA

SUMMARY

Our ancestors understood that the plants and animals that visit us—in our imaginations, dreams, or our waking lives—have messages for us. As we have covered, acupressure points provide direct access for natural energies to enter our gemfire chakra and release what we're ready to let go of. The frequencies of the third chakra are available through the rising sun and specific flowers in nature. And how fun to enjoy a mudra, a symbolic gesture that connects you to ancient times, all with the goal of activating your inner sun—your cheery solar plexus self.

7

SELF-HEALING AND GROUNDING

AMELIA VOGLER

I am a soul healer. I answer the fundamental questions about how to stay close to your inner light. I work with individuals to help them feel whole again, especially after they have shut down part of themselves. The energies of healthy, balanced personal power are an essential element of wholeness. Without a connection to your healthy power, there is no way to organize yourself in life. You float around directionless, without a healthy expression of your will. The energies of the solar plexus help you dare to create your dreams while honoring the dreams of others as equally sacred.

This chapter dives into practices to support the relationship between your soul and its power (or will), which lies in the ability to manage your thoughts and information. Here you will ground yourself as a healer through expanding the core foundations of self-healing and awaken the balanced potential of your third chakra through both hands-on and experiential practices.

As an example, Joe, a client of mine, was one of my best teachers about the third chakra. He had an unshakable will, and when I met him he was overwhelmed with his life. Some might call him selfish or self-centered as well as anxious and reactive. He had been traumatized by three life-threatening accidents, but despite that heavy layer of trauma, I could see the light in him immediately. Somewhere below that forcefulness he was gentle, loving, and determined in his self-healing.

He had all the ingredients for a healthy solar plexus. He was focused, strong-willed, interested in new information, and connected to his power, but all of these qualities were exaggerated. We worked together for about six years, slowly bringing the stuck energies of trauma back into flow, consistently returning to grounding and self-love practices. Today, Joe partners with the world around him. He is in his power but not powering over others. He still has outbursts of rage, but he catches them. He tends toward anxiety but is softer and less reactive than before. Joe expresses that he is living an everyday life now. He can dream and think of the future with an open mind and compassionate heart. Joe is living in a balanced expression of his third chakra. He can hear his soul again—a soul that is celebrating being alive.

FOUNDATIONS FOR SELF-HEALING

If there is one key to self-healing to take from working with the first and second chakras—whether or not you've read the previous books in this series that cover those—I'd say it is to refrain from needing to know everything that is mysterious. Let it be.

The next lesson of healing, encapsulated in your third chakra, is to engage your will. Your will is your unique and divine force or power. There is nothing you need to do to engage your will other than affirm that you are an exceptional being brought here to create and experience life through the alchemy of your gifts and perspective. To engage your will is to affirm yourself as powerful. The third chakra allows your will to be done. Begin each healing session by grounding in your "enoughness." You can then empower your healing intention with your willingness to be a catalyst for change. By engaging your will, you channel your expression of divine power.

PRACTICE

BALANCING YOUR THIRD
CHAKRA AND AURIC FIELD

Even though your third auric field is an extension of your third chakra, it can have a life of its own. Not every kind of energy makes its way through the auric field's lovely and protective sheath into the corresponding chakra (and vice versa), so it's important to allow them to integrate, which this practice will assist you in doing.

Preparation

Find a quiet and welcoming space for this exercise. Employ the personal practices in your toolkit, such as deep breathing and mindful focus, to steady and clear your mind of chatter. If you have a naturally chatty mind, try extending your exhale longer than your inhale for a few breath cycles. If you like, bring paper and pen to journal or process through writing. If you are a lover of color or art, gather paper and colored pencils.

Intention

To employ your intuitive abilities to experience the qualities of your third chakra and associated auric field, and use universal energies—energies available to all—to balance that chakra.

This practice is purely energetic; knowing why or understanding the story behind how this chakra is expressed is unnecessary. Instead, trust what you notice, and know that these universal energies support your balance.

Steps

» Sit or lie in any position that feels comfortable.

» Close your eyes or soften your gaze.

» Place your palms on your upper abdomen and, with intention, access your third chakra and auric field.

» Ask Creator or Spirit to bring forth universal energies to clear and balance your third chakra. These energies will remove unneeded energies and bring new complementary ones.

» Allow this balanced expression of your third chakra and auric field to integrate. Take some notes, journal, or draw to help you process any shifts.

PRACTICE

CLEARING THE SOLAR PLEXUS
WITH A SUN WALK

This is one of my absolute favorite personal solar plexus practices. It's an exercise I stumbled upon during one of the darkest, most sunless periods of my life.

Traumas have a way of bringing forth related energy patterns. In this case, I went down the rabbit hole of experiencing a sense of not feeling like I was enough.

The good news is that this present-day event triggered older traumas in such a way that I was resourced enough to see them clearly. Of course, I was overwhelmed by the self-deprecating patterns of my old wounds. For nights, I couldn't sleep. My mind, like a scratched record, replayed thoughts that did not serve me. My body was anxious and unsettled, my nervous system's way of telling me that I was disconnected from my divine will and truth.

My third chakra and auric field looked as though they were cloudy with dust. The brilliant yellow energy that generally radiated from my third chakra was held tightly to my body. My inner sun wasn't shining. My battery had been drained by trying to digest heavy thoughts. Then one moonless predawn morning, the ocean, a familiar healer in my life, called out to me. Determined to let the sea and salt soothe me, I went to the beach. It was warm outside, and I was alone. This particular beach runs east to west. I walked east toward the sun as the sky softened to dark blue and the horizon shone a light pink. As the sun crested the horizon, I felt that solar energy burning through the energies that were held in the front of my energy body. I could see the sunlight clearing my field and the bright yellow color returning.

I had a profound moment of remembering who I really was: someone who was worthy because she had been gifted this day. As the front of my energy field cleared, the back began to feel heavy and achy. The old stuck energies of those early-life traumas were responding to the reorganization of my own inner light.

Guided, I turned my back to the sun and walked back home intending to clear those patterns from the past. I classify the result as one of my life's miracles, as during that journey I walked myself back home to my will to be the one and only me.

Preparation

Wait for a nice bright day for this energy-clearing ritual.

You may walk at sunrise or during the daytime. If you are feeling emotional, consider performing your sun walk in the late afternoon when the light is soft and gentle.

Intention

To help burn away heavy thoughtforms or unhelpful beliefs from the present and the past.

Steps

» Sit quietly in meditation or intentional thought and sincerely connect with your personal spirit. Ask it to offer you information about your sense of personal power or will. You might ask, "What are the thoughts that stream from the parts of me that feel small or disempowered [or fill in your own experience]?" Because energy follows thoughts, these energies will naturally become more present and accessible. If you start to feel heavier, do not worry. At the perfect time, these energies will clear.

» As you begin to walk toward the sun, set an intention that the sun will clear the present and future energies held in your solar plexus and third auric field.

» Feel, sense, and experience the sun's warmth as it clears the energies.

» When the front of your energy feels lighter, turn and walk back toward where you started.

» Feel, sense, and experience the sun's warmth as it clears the energies.

» When you arrive at where you first started, again sit quietly in meditation or intentional thought and sincerely connect with your spirit. Ask that it offer you information about your sense of personal will.

PRACTICE

GROUNDING IN THE INTEGRITY OF YOU: A SOLAR PLEXUS AFFIRMATION

For years I have written healing affirmations, and in 2019 I embarked on a project with three gifted musicians to write music to accompany my affirmations for the chakras. The result was a beautiful album called *I Am I: Affirmations for Well Living, Whole Being, and the Emanation of Your Divine Inner Authority*, a compilation of twelve healing affirmations, with one for each chakra. Affirmations are energies that, when repeated, create new patterns in your energy body. Because form follows energy, affirmations support your energy rebalancing around new higher-vibrational or better-aligned patterns with your true self. I always loved the affirmation for the solar plexus chakra, so I offer it here as a practice.

Preparation

Before beginning, take a moment to breathe, settle, and ground yourself.

Intention

To bring new patterns into your solar plexus to inform the integrity of your personal truth.

Steps

» From that grounded place, slowly read the following affirmation:

In the sunrise of this moment, I am open and receptive to silencing the rusty clamor of my worn-out fears. A strong and clear breeze sweeps through, a lull and hush settle, and now I can hear the resounding messages of my virtues; I am a symphony of powerful voices. I stand in my integrity with ease, knowing that I am conducted only by my truth.

» Allow the energies to rearrange around the connection to your truth.

PRACTICE

RELEASING ANGER TO ACCESS YOUR WILLPOWER

As you endeavor to come to the power aspect of your will, sometimes it is necessary to name and work with your feelings first. Your feelings, especially anger, can block your personal power from flowing. By nature, anger wants to be transferred, but when it's held and stuck, it creates a block, like a cork in a champagne bottle.

This is a simple somatic (body-based) practice that can help move anger out of the energy body. I'm grateful to my teacher Heather for sharing it with me.

Preparation

Get in touch with your anger. Feel, sense, and acknowledge it. Allow yourself to notice how it shows up in your body.

Intention

To uncork anger from the body so the energies of the third chakra can reestablish a healthy flow.

Steps

» As you get in touch with your anger, observe what comes up. What are the sensations like? Do you feel a specific temperature? Do you notice any thoughts, images, or emotions arriving?

» Meet your anger with compassion and care.

» Stand in front of a wall or a closed door with your arms outstretched and place your palms on the surface.

» Push against the surface as hard as you can (you can even scream if you want) and let that energy move through your body.

» At the end of this practice, you may feel tired. That's okay. In the space you've created, this is where your divine will returns.

SUMMARY

The third chakra is where you digest life and connect to your own sense of personal power. These practices allow you to connect to the solar light beyond and within you to regain a balanced expression of your will forces. Using these practices will help you get in touch with your soul's capacity to show up in life and share the unique love that you are with the world.

8

GUIDED MEDITATIONS

AMANDA HUGGINS

We store much of our self-identification energy within the third chakra: our concept of self, belief in self, and trust in self. Our solar plexus is also the grounded seat of our intuition. Of course, we receive intuitive guidance from our upper chakras, but the third energy center is where we first feel our intuitive knowing in our bodies. It's our gut instinct.

When the solar plexus is out of balance, that connection to our gut instinct, or intuition, becomes muddled. We begin to ask *Is this my intuition or am I just anxious right now?* Separating anxiety from intuition is a common and often perplexing journey, but it is one that can be supported through meditation.

Sitting with the breath is one way to still the mind and clear out the energy that obstructs the ability to clearly receive guidance from the third chakra. Not only does meditation help dissipate blocks, stories, and fears, but it offers an opportunity to reaffirm your inner sense of power and trust in self.

MEDITATING AND CONNECTING WITH THE THIRD CHAKRA

The meditations in this chapter will bring you through a process of separating anxiety from intuition to ultimately land with a deeper sense of confidence, trust, and connection to your personal power.

The first meditation is a practice for clearing out stories and connecting with your solar plexus. Through your breath and visualization, you will release energies that prevent you from connecting to your true, empowered self. You will also sit in loving, nonjudgmental observation of the solar plexus, familiarizing yourself with this energy center and charging and expanding it.

The second meditation builds upon that work of clearing and charging your gemfire chakra, using visualization to draw in and increase your sense of personal power. You will also offer the subconscious mind trust- and confidence-building affirmations to reprogram your beliefs about yourself. Affirmation, or mantra work, is an important tool when you're building new belief systems: when you're more relaxed (in the alpha brainwave state), the subconscious mind is more receptive to new information. Breathing in or infusing yourself with statements like "I am worthy," "I trust myself," and "I am powerful" while in meditation allows the truth of those words to sink deeply into your mind, body, and energetic system.

The third meditation, another visualization exercise, is a guided journey where you will channel direction about your personal power, confidence, and sense of self. You'll get to practice creating and visualizing from an empowered, intuitive space.

These meditations can be practiced on their own and in any order, but I suggest starting with the first meditation and practicing it for a few days before moving on to the next. It may also be helpful to read through the meditations in full first so you can practice the visualizations without having to open your eyes and refer back to the instructions. I also encourage you to make these meditations your own. The scripts presented below are simply guidelines; it is a beautiful exercise in trust to lead yourself through a practice that feels right for you. There's no wrong way to do it.

As with all meditative practices, remember that it's perfectly fine to still have thoughts or feel distracted. When that happens, simply take a cleansing breath and mindfully refocus your attention on the solar plexus.

PRACTICE

CLEARING, OPENING, AND
CHARGING THE THIRD CHAKRA

To begin this meditation, find a comfortable seated position with spine upright and shoulders soft. You may place your hands face-down on your thighs to connect with yourself and your sense of power, or you may choose to place one or both hands on or above the belly button area for direct connection with the solar plexus.

Begin taking deep, calm, easy breaths in and out through the nose. Give yourself a few cycles of deep breathing to simply connect with your body. Notice any spaces in the physical body that feel tight or stuck or like they're holding on to something.

Imagine sinking an anchor down from the base of your spine deeply into and through the cushion beneath you and all the way into the core of the earth.

In your mind's eye see a cord glowing with white light dropping down from high in the sky and connecting with the crown of your head. Allow this upper cord and your grounding cord to move through the spinal column and merge with each other, meeting at your third chakra.

Continuing to take deep breaths, simply allow the white light at your third chakra to radiate to and through every cell, muscle, and fiber of your body. Next, see that light extending beyond the physical body and out into the space around you. Take note of how far this light travels.

Allow that healing, protective light to remain there as you draw your focus back to the solar plexus.

Now examine this energy center: a brilliant sunny yellow light spinning counterclockwise. Notice what you observe. Without judging it, notice the chakra's size, speed of spin, and vibrancy.

Then ask this chakra to show you what stands in the way of your wholeness. You may ask to be shown energy of anxiety, fear, doubt, or lack of trust. Ask that the chakra show you these energies as a color. Observe the color you see and where it shows up within this chakra. For example, you may see splotches of muddy green or a layer of spiky, textured black energy. You do not need to label or go into specifics of what you are being shown; just notice and receive.

Next, visualize a clear bubble forming about four feet in front of you, outside your auric field and directly across from your solar plexus.

As you continue to breathe, move the energy sitting in your solar plexus into that bubble. See it fill up with the colors, textures, and vibrations you observed until the bubble is full. If needed, you can create multiple bubbles.

When you feel you have cleared out the energy, visualize a matchstick or stick of dynamite being placed underneath the bubble(s). Explode the energy and watch as your blockages break up into tiny pieces and are reabsorbed by the universe.

Observe your third chakra once more. Notice any physical or energetic changes you're experiencing. Enjoy how the body, mind, and spirit feel when the anxious energy has been released and your channel of connection is clearer. Notice just how grounded you feel and how you like that sensation.

Notice the health of this chakra now. Assess whether or not the speed of rotation has increased or if the sunny gold seems more bright or bold. Spend a few breaths in conscious observation, bringing the chakra to a speed, vibrancy, and size that feels empowering for you.

When you are ready, offer a gentle inner thank-you to your spirit, your guides, and the universe before coming out of your meditation.

Be sure to drink water after you get up from your meditation seat; you will have moved quite a bit of energy.

PRACTICE

AFFIRMING YOUR PERSONAL POWER AND SENSE OF TRUST

Start by taking deep breaths to ground into the body. Take at least five minutes, if not longer, to soften into a state of deep physical relaxation. This is a space in which you will receive.

Direct your attention to the solar plexus. Tune in to the speed of rotation, size, and vibrancy of this chakra.

Visualize grounding down from your third chakra with an energetic cord. As this cord roots into the earth beneath you, see it branch off into hundreds of smaller pathways (much like the roots of a tree or fibers of a neural network). See those roots multiplying even more, extending downward, left to right, expanding far and wide.

Just as the roots of a tree draw in water from the earth for their nourishment, these energetic roots draw in personal power and energy for *your* system.

For three cycles of breath, see, feel, and imagine drawing a brilliant yellow light upward through these roots and into your solar plexus. You are bringing up confidence.

Take three more cycles of slow deep breathing as you pull up the energy of personal power.

Take three more cycles of breath to draw in a sense of trust in the self and in your knowing.

Throughout this portion of the practice, use your exhalations to release any energies of anxiety, shame, fear, or self-doubt. See that energy being released through the roots and reabsorbed by the earth.

Pause.

On your next inhale, affirm to yourself *I trust myself*. As you exhale, release any energy that disputes this affirmation.

Inhale *I am worthy*. Exhale to release unworthiness.

Inhale *I am allowed to take up space*. Exhale to release self-minimization.

Inhale *I trust my inner knowing*. Exhale to release anxiety.

Inhale *I am confident in who I am today and who I am becoming*. Exhale to release self-doubt and judgment.

Inhale *I own my power*. Exhale to release shame.

Continue on, intuitively creating your affirmations to suit the power-filled narrative you are building for yourself. As you breathe into these affirmations, practice creating the feelings and emotions associated with each statement. Embrace what taking up space feels like in your body and what it's like to be confident and trusting in yourself.

When you are ready to close the meditation, take note of any positive feelings and emotions you were able to conjure up in the body and hold them within you.

Take a final deep inhalation to seal the positive energy you have called in.

Release that breath with a deep exhale and open your eyes, keeping any feelings of confidence, personal power, or trust with you for as long as you can.

PRACTICE

THE SUNNY DAY MEDITATION TO CONNECT WITH YOUR PERSONAL POWER

Place yourself in a comfortable position, either seated or lying down, and bring both hands to rest on your solar plexus.

Direct your attention to the breath. Breathe smoothly, softly, and deeply for about three to five minutes.

Bring your awareness into your third chakra. Imagine yourself seated comfortably in the very center of this space, surrounded by brilliant yellow light. Notice how safe, calm, and joyful it feels to rest in this space. As you sit in the center of this chakra and look around, you see that this brilliant light extends infinitely above, below, and all around you.

The space you're in transforms, and you see yourself sitting on a blanket in a beautiful field. It is pleasantly warm, the sun is drenching you in a beautifully soft light, and you're surrounded by wild sunflowers. Observe what else shows up in this imaginal space.

Your body feels safe here. *You* are safe here—safe to be yourself, safe to take up space, safe to trust your inner knowing. In this place there is no anxiety or fear, only trust and a deep appreciation for who you are.

You reach into a basket next to you and take out a leather journal. See yourself writing down a date—a date in the future—and watch as your pencil writes the sentence *I am so proud of who I am because . . .*

Watch as you continue to write and finish that prompt. Allow the you within this power-filled space to write down your inner truths, and take note of what comes through.

You finish that prompt and smile. It feels good to be who you are and where you are right now.

In fact, that feeling inspires another thought. You pick up the pencil once more and write *I am so grateful that I learned to trust myself. I built that sense of inner trust by . . .*

Perceive how this version of you built a deep sense of trust. It exhibits no need to question or analyze what comes up; it merely breathes and observes the guidance that has emerged from this energy center.

See yourself smile as you write fervently and with a sense of loving pride for your growth. Before closing the journal, this future self writes down one last thing: *If I could go back in time and tell myself the truth about my own power, I would say*. . . Observe and receive the positive words of encouragement and affirmation.

See yourself close the journal and place it back into the basket. Own the sense of wholeness, completion, and trust.

Breathe deeply and bask in these feelings for as long as you'd like. When you're ready to return to your body, take three cycles of energizing breaths and gently blink your eyes open.

SUMMARY

Meditation has been used for thousands of years to create inner calm, clear jangling nerves, and open us to a better future. In this chapter you participated in three meditations to activate and soothe your third chakra. Know that you can use them as often as you desire.

9

VIBRATIONAL REMEDIES

JO-ANNE BROWN

Ideally, our healthy third chakra energies are established in early childhood, but if this doesn't happen, it's not too late. Our third chakra can be empowered at later stages of life through subtle energy support.

In this chapter I will enhance your understanding of vibrational remedies for the third chakra by:

- » explaining what they are

- » describing their benefits

- » elaborating on both support-based and tangible remedies

- » sharing my preferred third chakra remedies with you

- » outlining two practices to support your third chakra at home

As an example of the effectiveness of these remedies for working with your third chakra, I am going to introduce Ursula, a client of mine. She employed me years ago when she was suffering from exhaustion, digestive issues, and sugar cravings. Despite her lack of energy, she had big dreams and aspirations. Although Ursula had a strong work ethic, the messaging she had received from her birth family was that she wasn't enough and didn't belong.

As with many people who are deficient in healthy third chakra energies, she suffered from parasitic overload, a classic energetic indicator that her personal boundaries were being breached.

We worked with vibrational remedies to validate her third chakra, support her spleen and pancreas, and clear the parasites affecting other third chakra organs.

Under challenging circumstances Ursula completed postgraduate studies while ensuring that her children had a myriad of educational and social experiences. She is now able to set clear boundaries with her family of origin and maintains healthy relationships with her nuclear family and friends. Her professional talents and intelligence are valued, and she generously supports her local community.

WHAT ARE VIBRATIONAL REMEDIES?

Vibrational remedies are restorative practices or medicines. When they are specifically created to support the third chakra, they validate our unique essence, enabling us to reach our personal and professional potential.

When there is disharmony within our solar plexus chakra, we can experience a lack of self-worth and a reticence to fully show up in the world. We can become reactive, anxious, and indecisive as we desperately seek approval externally that we can't find within ourselves.

For both the third chakra and its physical counterparts, balance and harmony occur when personal empowerment is attained or restored.

WHAT IS RESONANCE?

Resonance is a phenomenon present within all vibrational remedies. It occurs when an object responds (or vibrates) at the same natural frequency as a secondary object.

Consider two tuning forks, both attuned to the same musical note. When the first tuning fork is sounded, the second one also starts to vibrate. It produces the same sound because the two instruments share the same energy and information. When this occurs, they are in vibrational alignment; they are resonating.

Our chakras work in the same way. When healthy third chakra remedies are introduced to us, they catalyze positive change. Our third chakra resonates with the remedy's self-regulating energies and synchronizes with them as a result of their shared energy and information.

THE ROLE OF THE SUN IN CREATING VIBRATIONAL REMEDIES

In part 1 we learned that the solar plexus chakra is aligned with the sun. In astrology our sun sign represents our identity, the essence we radiate into the world. In the same way, vibrational remedies for the third chakra allow us to more easily express our vital energy into the world.

One of two preferred methods for creating flower-based vibrational remedies is the sun method, where flowers are gathered and placed in glass bowls of pure water in the sunlight. The sun's energy then infuses or imprints the vibrational essence of the flower into the liquid medium of water.

This isn't the sun's first encounter with the flowers. Through the process of photosynthesis, the sun's energy has already created the flowering plants' food source, glucose. The solar plexus chakra empowers action and thinking, as does glucose. This process is aided by the mitochondria (subcellular factories) in the plant cells, which create energy for growth and repair.

As humans, we also have mitochondria in our cells: powerhouses that produce energy and heat. Like our solar plexus chakra, which filters our helpful from harmful thoughts and ideas, our mitochondria also have a discerning role: to distinguish between healthy and unhealthy cells in our bodies.

Given the discerning role of the third chakra, it therefore should come as no surprise that it is often described as the mitochondria of the chakra system.

Just as the sun affirms our personal energy through our mitochondria and our third chakra, it also affirms and imprints life-energy patterns of flowers into the watery medium that forms the basis of the mother tincture of a flower essence.

VIBRATIONAL REMEDIES
FOR OUR THIRD CHAKRA

Vibrational remedies fall into one of two categories:

» support-based remedies

» tangible remedies

Support-Based Vibrational Remedies

Support-based vibrational remedies include subtle energy treatments, therapies, and practices that can require the guidance of a qualified practitioner. They support our gem-fire chakra energies through:

> » skin-to-skin contact (including acupuncture and massage)

> » vibrational media (including color therapies, frequency-based modalities, sound therapy, and qigong)

> » demonstrational guidance (including eye movement desensitization and reprocessing [EMDR] and yoga)

I will now highlight in greater detail four modalities that are extremely effective for third chakra fortification.

Three of these methods are vibrational media: sound therapies, frequency-based therapies, and qigong. The fourth modality, EMDR, falls under the category of demonstrative guidance.

SOUND THERAPIES. Research has shown that supportive frequencies for the third chakra are in the range of 349 Hz to 440 Hz. I frequently work with 396 Hz, one of three solfeggio frequencies that relate to the conscious mind plane (the other two being 639 Hz and 963 Hz).

Many vibrational practitioners also use the 528 Hz frequency to support the third chakra. While this isn't my personal choice, I find this frequency is beneficial for all chakras.

FREQUENCY-BASED THERAPIES. These therapies employ the use of simple low-voltage frequency-generating devices to direct therapeutic vibrations to the body through conductive electrodes. The most well-known of these devices is the Rife machine.

When the body receives the generated vibrations during a therapy session, the vibrations allow the third chakra organ systems to self-regulate. This is achieved through either the activation or calming of specific organs and meridians as described in traditional Chinese medicine (TCM).

For example, two frequencies (60 Hz and 127 kHz) can be used to stimulate any of the points along the spleen/pancreas meridian, allowing the release of blocked energies.

Frequency-based therapies specific to other third chakra meridians (small intestines, liver, and gallbladder) can also be used.

THE SIX HEALING SOUNDS. *Liu Zi Jue* is one form of Chinese qigong; it is a movement-based practice that has been used for many centuries to promote *qi*, or energy.

Two of these healing sounds support the third chakra yin organs, the spleen and the liver. Later in this chapter, you will find a step-by-step healing practice outlining how to use these two healing sounds.

EYE MOVEMENT DESENSITIZATION AND REPROCESSING (EMDR). This structured technique is helpful for reducing the effects of trauma, anxiety-related disorders, and other third chakra imbalances.

During a guided therapy session, the patient focuses on a negative event and simultaneously experiences bilateral stimulation (through eye movements, lighting, tones, taps, or vibrations) to activate both sides of the brain.

This method calms the amygdala (the brain's fear center) and allows reconsolidation of previously acquired memories in a way that is non traumatizing for most people.

Tangible Vibrational Remedies

Tangible vibrational remedies are literally energetic infusions or "medicines" stored in readily available carriers for speedy ingestion and absorption. These carriers include liquid (water- and alcohol-based), pills and pilules, and oils, ointments, and salves. Essential oils are more typically diffused into the air, influencing our energetic system through our sense of smell.

HOMEOPATHIC REMEDIES. Homeopathy is a system of resonance-based medicine centered on the law of similars, which states the substance that triggers disease or dysfunction can be used to treat that same disease or dysfunction.

During diagnosis, practitioners prescribe a suitable remedy at an appropriate potency to invoke a healing response in the patient.

Given that the third chakra has a mental focus, discernment must be used when working with homeopathic remedies. When the principal symptoms are physical (such as digestive issues), lower-potency remedies (6C or 30C) are recommended. However, if the symptoms are more mentally, emotionally, or cognitively based (such as anxiety or depression), a qualified practitioner would typically prescribe a higher-potency remedy.

Homeopathic remedies that promote healthy third chakra energies include Argentum Nitricum (for nervous system support), Lycopodium (for low self-esteem), Nux Vomica (for digestive support), and Cina Maritima (for parasite cleansing and mental/emotional imbalances).

FLOWER ESSENCES. One of the earliest advocates for flower essences was Hildegard von Bingen, a twelfth-century Benedictine abbess who used muslin cloths to collect dew drops from flowering plants to treat people with emotional imbalances.

While many high-integrity flower essences are available, here I'm featuring essences with the solar plexus qualities and benefits I've personally experienced and witnessed.

» *Australian Bushflower Essences.* This range of flower-based remedies was formulated by Ian White, a fifth-generation Australian herbalist. Australian bushflower remedies for the third chakra include Focus Essence (for clarity, focus, and integration of ideas), Calm & Clear

Essence (for clarity and recognition of personal needs), Confid Essence (for confidence and personal power), Bush Fuchsia (for problem solving and trust of one's gut feelings), and Paw Paw (for assimilation of new ideas).

» *Elementals Flower Essence Range*. This range of flower essences was created by US-based acupuncturist and author Lindsay Fauntleroy, who is the featured author of chapter 6. She describes her essence range as nature allies that support energetic healing. Three of her essences, which are not mentioned in Lindsay's chapter, support the solar plexus chakra: Fire: Wholehearted (for empowerment and courage), Wood: Stand (for personal power, energy, and liver/ gallbladder support), and Earth: Manifest (for mental focus and pancreatic support). You can find these essences on Lindsay's website, www.ElementalsEssences.com.

» *HeartRadiance Essence Range*. This range of Australian wildflower essences was created by Annie Meredith, renowned chakra healer, to share the inherent, life-giving wisdom of the flowers with others, especially women. Her Manipura Essence enables the solar plexus chakra qualities of personal empowerment, easy decision making, and digestive balance.

Following are two vibrational practices to support your third chakra.

PRACTICE

HEALING SOUNDS FOR
THE SOLAR PLEXUS CHAKRA

The Six Healing Sounds from qigong are six different forms of exhaled breathing that "create resonance" in our bodies. Two of these healing sounds specifically support the third chakra yin organs, the spleen and liver, and create resonance within our third chakras.

For the Spleen

» Take three deep breaths in and out, and place your left hand on your third chakra.

» Breathe in and visualize yellow, the color that represents the spleen in TCM.

» Breathe out the spleen healing sound, pronounced *Whooo*, in a guttural tone. Visualize this outward breath as coming from your spleen, on the left side of your third chakra.

» Breathe out and visualize unhealthy energies of worry and obsessive thinking being released from your spleen. Feel those energies being replaced by a sense of calm and trust.

For the Liver

» Take three deep breaths in and out, and place your right hand on your third chakra.

» Breathe in and visualize green, the color that represents the liver in TCM.

» Breathe out the liver healing sound, pronounced *Shhhh*, the calming sound you would make when reassuring a baby. Visualize this outward breath as coming from your liver, on the right side of your third chakra.

» Breathe out and visualize unhealthy energies of anger and frustration being released from your liver. Feel those energies being replaced by a sense of confidence and courage.

PRACTICE

CREATE YOUR OWN THIRD CHAKRA VIBRATIONAL REMEDY

» Draw the third chakra yantra as depicted in yellow on page i.

» Take a glass of filtered water and place it on top of the yantra.

» From the top of the glass, view the symbol through the water.

» Request that all the third chakra attributes you desire be infused into your water through the third chakra yantra symbol.

» Place the glass of filtered water (with the yantra symbol beneath it) in the sunlight for ten minutes to allow full realization of your intentions, knowing the sun's energy will imprint the water with your desired third chakra qualities.

» Drink the filtered water, visualizing that you are receiving your chosen third chakra attributes.

SUMMARY

Vibrational remedies cleanse and activate our energies. Through powerful third chakra remedies, we can tap into our dynamic solar plexus core in a most empowered and transformative way.

This chapter includes several remedies and practices to support you in your third chakra development. Now that you've learned about them, show some love to manipura, the sunny energy center that helps you embrace your own intelligence and personal power, and step out with confidence.

10

CRYSTALS, MINERALS, AND STONES

MARGARET ANN LEMBO

Confidence, mental clarity, personal power, and high self-esteem sum up the key energies of the solar plexus chakra. The third chakra is the center for your ability to take in, absorb, and integrate life. Using crystals, minerals, and stones for chakra balance and alignment is a perfect reminder of your intentions and helps you gain clarity. These precious gifts of the earth bring sparkle, shine, and vibrant color to your spiritual journey.

The solar plexus chakra is the powerhouse that will help you stand in your power. It is the part of your consciousness responsible for digesting life as well as food and nutrition, and it is your reminder that anything you put your attention into can manifest.

In your physical body, the solar plexus chakra is located between your heart and your navel, just above your belly button. The primary color associated with the solar plexus chakra is yellow as well as shades of green such as olive, emerald, forest, and chartreuse. The solar plexus chakra connects your magnificence and unlimited potential. The gemstones from Mother Earth, mainly colored with fire-gem hues and serving the third chakra's higher purposes, are allies and tools for your time here on this planet.

THE POWER OF INTENTION

When working with third chakra gems, focus on the desired experience. Whatever you focus on becomes your reality. All your conscious thoughts and feelings—as well as the subconscious and unconscious ones—have created your current life. This basic principle is at the heart of most universal laws, including the laws of attraction and physics. I was taught these basic principles at a very young age. In my work with color and crystals for over three decades, I've found that a stone is most effective when associated with an intention.

It's easy to choose the perfect stone to match your intention. Simply focus on the image or thought of your intention, then look at the choices of crystals available to you, either in a store or in your private collection. Here I'll provide my recommendations on which stones to use, but trust your inner guidance too. If you are attracted to a gemstone while choosing crystals, go with your gut and what is attractive to you. Match your positive thought with that gemstone and watch your world realign. In the practice at the end of this chapter, you can use the stones I highlight here to support self-confidence, mental clarity, and digestion.

SELF CONFIDENCE

With a balanced solar plexus, you see and live in the world with joy, optimism, and a positive attitude. When you are filled with joy, it is easy to be enthusiastic, self-confident, and courageous. It takes courage to shine your light brightly and set boundaries with others, as core foundational beliefs about yourself are formed at a very young age.

It is important to shine your light because this encourages others to do the same. Becoming a role model is a selfless act, and it also assists your self-esteem.

Here are my go-to gemstones to amplify the positive.

Amber is beneficial in setting boundaries. As you heal, your former emotional state will try to suck you back into the familiar. Also, those around you may not be comfortable with your changes, as they might need to look at themselves. As you raise your consciousness and heal yourself, you break familial patterns of poor health, abusive behavior, addictive tendencies, or anything else that is not in alignment with love. You also provide the foundation and doorway for future generations of your family, including extended family, to gain benefits from your self-healing. The work you do to heal yourself and make yourself a better person is an unselfish act, as many others benefit when you raise your consciousness. Amber affirmations include these: *My energy is protected from the thoughts and feelings of others. I realize when I need to be discerning about the people in my circle. I am very grateful for the mutual respect of the people around me.*

Citrine is the yellow variety of quartz (crystalline silicon dioxide). Citrine activates self-confidence and joy. Use this stone to ease depression and relieve feelings of inferiority or unworthiness. The radiant vibration citrine emits can remind you about joy, peace, and love. Let the golden rays of this stone dissipate whatever challenge or negative emotion is blocking your way to happiness. Good for mental clarity, citrine reminds you that whatever you ardently believe, desire, and work passionately toward will manifest. Use this stone to awaken your awareness and become conscious of the repetitive patterns of self-limiting thoughts that are holding you back. Repeat affirmations like these: *I am brave and have high self-esteem. I allow others to see me and all my goodness. I emanate goodness and light.*

Golden calcite is calcium carbonate that crystallizes in a rhombohedral system. Golden calcite aids you in transitioning from one way of being to another. With its sparkling golden light, it illuminates your path while sorting out feelings and releasing the fear of change. Use it to remember your magnificence. Your light will shine so brightly that it will be immediately recognizable. Golden calcite is also an excellent stone for bolstering optimism and centering you in your personal power. With a strong sense of yourself, you can achieve anything you want employing affirmations like these: *I acknowledge my worth. I set boundaries with others when necessary. It is beneficial for me and others when I radiate my light. I have high self-esteem.*

MENTAL CLARITY AND AWAKENED AWARENESS

Your third chakra is your source of joy, happiness, and situational awareness. With a balanced solar plexus, you see things in a positive light and absorb all that life offers. The following stones will aid in these endeavors.

Malachite, a hydrated copper carbonate, can clear your mind and help you observe the patterns of your consciousness. Gaze at malachite when too many thoughts are circulating in your head. That practice will realign your mind with your heart and solar plexus. Allow malachite's swirling shades of green to reveal the lessons involved in a tough situation; you can use this wisdom to further your spiritual evolution. As you discover which practices no longer serve you, remove them and replace them with new habits. Look for emerging patterns of joy, harmony, and inner peace. Embrace them and continue forward in your evolutionary spiral upward with affirmations such as these: *I have a heart-centered awareness. I practice love, compassion, and kindness every day. I perceive recurring patterns and use the knowledge for the highest good.*

Amethyst and **ametrine** are excellent for changing a situation. Purple is the opposite of yellow on the color wheel, and that color will aid you in friendship troubles and powerlessness. Gain the ability to impact an outcome by employing visualization and your imagination while embedded in the energy of purple that swirls in amethyst. This process is especially beneficial if someone around you is being a bully and you need to increase your confidence and courage.

Ametrine contains the complementary colors of purple and yellow. The purple transforms and transmutes negative emotions and releases the hooks that others have in your emotional body. The yellow encourages the ability to discern which people, places, and situations to allow into your life, aiding you in courageously setting boundaries when needed. Use affirmations such as these: *Life is magical. I use my imagination to create a better way of being. I am blessed with goodness and love.*

INTEGRATION AND DIGESTION

The energy vibrating at the solar plexus chakra is associated with feeling balanced and in control of situations. Within this basin you deal with feelings of being overwhelmed and powerlessness. Check to see how you are metaphorically swallowing and processing what is happening in your world. You want to notice if it's too much or if you feel deprived in some way.

The solar plexus is the part of your consciousness that processes all life has to offer. It is the area where most digestion takes place, so it relates to how you absorb and access food and all other aspects of reality. This sunny yellow chakra holds the vibration of joy and optimism or despair and pessimism. The choice is yours.

Apatite is a stone that is beneficial for digesting and absorbing what you need in order to maintain health, well-being, and balance on all levels. Work with apatite to help you understand your feelings. With its qualities of assimilation and absorption, apatite is a perfect stone to separate valid from invalid thoughts, especially those adding confusion to your life. Interact with this stone to integrate the events happening in your environment. Apatite also reminds you to pay attention to the food you are putting into your body and what you think or talk about while eating. Wholesome food, thoughts, and conversation can make things easier to process and accept. Try these affirmations: *I mentally, emotionally, and physically integrate what is happening in the world and in my inner life. I am good about noticing what is going on around me. I have a healthy digestive system.*

Trilobite is a fossil of marine creatures that flourished over 500 million years ago and have been extinct for over 250 million years. This fossil is ideal for aiding in filtering information to keep unwanted energies away from you or, at a minimum, away from your awareness. This ancient filtering system is useful when you need support in dealing with life's minutiae as well as your emotions. Figure out which feelings are yours and which have been imposed upon you by society or other people. It is a good fossil to use if you are empathic and take on other people's feelings and emotions. Discern what's best for you and choose to be strong and aligned with your highest good with affirmations like these: *My digestive system is excellent at filtering anything that isn't beneficial to me. I understand and process my life experiences.*

Peridot helps transform negative emotions like jealousy, self-sabotage, agitation, and impatience into lighter emotions such as love, compassion, acceptance, and gratitude. It is also beneficial to assist you in digesting life—accepting your world as it is and then transforming it with clear intention to create the reality you desire. Peridot supports the digestive system, assuring the optimal functioning of the gallbladder, liver, pancreas, and spleen. This olive-colored stone also supports the proper assimilation of nutrients from food, drink, water, and light. Stay focused on the goodness in your life and employ this stone to calm the nervous energy around the solar plexus and stomach area while warding off negativity and jealousy, both internally and externally. Remove your attention from others' good fortune and focus on the blessings in your own life, and step away from people who are resentful of your destiny. This transformative gem gives you the inner strength to transcend any challenges. Use it to open your mind to unlimited possibilities with affirmations like these: *The people in my circle are happy about the blessings in my life. I place my focus on my good fortune. I know that good thoughts and good actions bring good results.*

PRACTICE

STONES FOR SELF-CONFIDENCE, MENTAL CLARITY, AND DIGESTION

Hold one or more of the stones highlighted above and compose an affirmation. Then imagine the sun shining at your solar plexus, warming you up and helping you receive all that life has to offer. You are worthy of all that is good. Use your imagination and bask in the brilliant yellow light.

SUMMARY

It is essential to cultivate your personal power through awareness. Your thoughts, words, and actions will strengthen your courage and self-confidence. Use the gems noted in this chapter when you need the guts to set boundaries and stand up for yourself. It is essential to set an intention and focus on the positive so that life reflects your highest potential. We create our lives with our thoughts, actions, words, and deeds. Your intentions vibrate into the world and return to you in the form of your reality. Take a grounded and optimistic approach with high self-esteem to design your reality.

11

MANTRA HEALING

BLAKE TEDDER

In this age of endless distraction and overwhelming amounts of information to process, focusing the mind and becoming clearheaded seem like almost superhuman feats—but they're not. There's a mantra that can help you with these concerns. In this chapter I'll explore the power of mantra to connect you with that radiant, confident, discriminating, and clear state of mind that emerges when your solar plexus chakra is expressed and in balance. I'll also introduce some practices to carry with you on your path toward healing, self-mastery, and freedom—practices that can work alongside the other exercises in this book.

The ancient power of mantra has been at the core of my decades-long healing journey. Early on in my study of yoga, sitting still in meditation and waiting for my mind to relax did not seem like an option for me. I had far too many thoughts, and they swirled at lightning speed. Because of my history of significant PTSD, there were times when constant anxiety, racing thoughts, and inner tension seemed insurmountable. Mantra practice gave me another way in. Repeating mantras aloud was physical, and it gave me something I could do in meditation. It quickly produced noticeable changes, ultimately making me more receptive to meditative states.

In fact, mantra became so important to me that I would go on to host an acclaimed international radio show and podcast dedicated to the call-and-response devotional chanting of mantras called *kirtan*. I led chanting groups and played in numerous mantra music groups. For some of us, once we discover the power of these phrases to clean the mind and produce different states of consciousness, we never look back.

WHAT IS A MANTRA?

Before we go any further, let's be clear about what mantras are not. They are not corporate slogans or succinct advice from a life coach. If a sentence starts with "Our mantra is. . . ," what's coming next is not a mantra. The word has been commodified, like "guru" and "karma," to indicate something similar but far less powerful. Mantra is a Sanskrit word combining *manas*, or "the thinking mind," and *trā*, or "instrument/tool." I like the translation "mind protector"—literally a tool you can use to make the mind resilient through its focused application.

Mantras in a religious context are primarily used in Hinduism, Buddhism, and Sikhism. They are sacred words, sounds, phrases, formulas, and names of deities that, in addition to focusing the mind, have special power that is stored in the ancient technology of the Sanskrit language. Many mantras have been chanted for thousands of years and have deep histories, delightful associated stories, devotional contexts, and protocols for intonation and pronunciation. While an understanding of these elements makes a given mantra much more potent, we can still gain tremendous benefit by just chanting the basic sounds.

MANTRAS AND THE POWER OF THOUGHTS

Most of us go about our worlds in a constant mental chatter, the fire of our minds set loose by the constantly changing winds of thought and experience. Try this short exercise as a warm-up to the practices in this chapter.

While sitting quietly, take five minutes and simply watch your mind. Observe how constantly you talk to yourself. In each successive moment arises a thought about what you like and dislike about a situation, what you want more of or less of, how an action or object reflects positively or negatively on you, what and whom you should bring closer or avoid altogether, or what went on in the past and what might happen in the future. It is utterly endless—and exhausting.

Now imagine that all this thinking energy could be drawn back into your belly to use for bodily processes like digestion, reinforcing energetic boundaries, and directing your life force. With a mind contained and not loosed to the winds, the fire of your third chakra has something to burn, and it can burn clean and at an appropriate temperature for any situation.

Why doesn't this happen automatically? Much of the mind's work is invested in seeking out patterns of pleasure and pain around us and producing conditions of relative safety and stability. The mind is extraordinary, but this primary and habitual tendency can be limiting to your potential for well-being. Think of how a comfort zone works. If you only live within your self-imposed and limiting beliefs, you will never approach your capacities for healing, happiness, transformation, and service. When you are not living fully because of limiting beliefs, trauma, emotional confusion, or any number of indignities that can befall a human being, the repetitive thoughts and stories you tell yourself are simply something your mind is doing to make sense of the situation and find some form of safety and stability. To our minds, it seems a more solid proposition to latch onto an arising thought than to experience what could be under the surface.

Think of riding in a crowded, swaying subway car. Imagine that despite all the jostling of passengers and bags and movement on the tracks, you could stand steady without holding on. Feel the activation required from your feet and legs and up into your belly. Feel the sense of security, confidence, and groundedness. When you are not connected to your lower chakras—feeling secure, creative, and empowered—you must grab onto something. Like the repetitive thoughts that are always floating above your embodied experience, the railing overhead in the crowded subway car is the easiest thing to grab for stability. It's not wrong; it's the best you can do.

The skillful use of mantra can be like a sleight-of-hand trick, taking advantage of the mind's tendency to latch onto thoughts. By replacing your habitual—and usually negative—thoughts with a new type of thoughtform using mantra, you can use your mind to outmaneuver your mind. It's a trip.

Since the solar plexus chakra is so linked with thoughts, mantra practice is a very powerful tool to help activate and balance this chakra. Let's explore some practices that will assist you with this.

START SIMPLY WITH THE ESSENCE

As you learned in part 1, each chakra has an associated Sanskrit syllable that can serve as a tool for activating and balancing that chakra. By repeating and invoking this *bija* mantra or "seed syllable" for each chakra, you create a connection and call it into expression. For the third chakra, the seed syllable is *Ram*, pronounced "rum" or "rahm."

Take a moment to sit in a quiet location where you will not be disturbed by external matters. Take a few deep, clearing breaths while consciously releasing as much tension as possible from your body. Sit up with a straight spine, ensuring that your chest and throat are open. Begin to warm up the vocal cords and diaphragm by exhaling with the long, reverberant sound of "ah" (the "a" pronounced as in the word "odd"). Try to source the sound from as deep in the belly as possible. Repeat ten times, feeling the vibration of the tone anywhere in the body that you can, paying special attention to your belly.

Now set a timer for five to ten minutes. Bring your awareness down to just behind your navel. Breathe in deeply, and chant *Ram* for the full length of the exhalation. Continue. As you proceed, maintain an erect spine but continue to soften the body. Feel the vibration of this bija mantra more and more deeply, like a vibrational seed being planted in your energy system. It can be very helpful to place your hands on your belly to guide your feeling there. When your timer goes off, take a moment to notice how you feel. Let whatever you feel register in your experience.

After a few sessions of vocalizing the bija mantra and seeding the sound into your energy system, try repeating the sound internally, without using your voice. When you get closely acquainted with it, you can practice this bija mantra at any time you want to invoke the power of your third chakra—even while you're engaged in a challenging conversation. It is very beneficial to use this bija mantra, externally or internally, while engaged in any of the yoga postures in this book.

PRACTICE

WORK WITH A TRADITIONAL MANTRA

Traditional mantras are more general in their scope than the above bija mantra and will benefit you in different ways, not just in your third chakra. Often the practices of particular mantras are tied to specific deities and devotional practices, and there are indeed traditional mantras that are associated with the element of fire, which will activate the fiery third chakra. Two simple mantras can be used to invoke qualities of the god of fire and the god of the sun.

Follow the same steps as in the first practice for preparing yourself, warming up the voice and opening the body. For this practice it can be powerful to have visualization aids. When practicing the fire mantra, light a candle or sit by a fire pit. For the sun mantra, sit in the midday sun if you are able, or receive the first light from the sun as it rises. These conditions will allow you to link the elemental power present in your direct experience with the elemental power in the mantras. If these scenarios are not available to you, then internally visualize a fire or the sun to support the chants.

In either case, create an inner desire to know and embody the element of fire in your belly. Depending on the mantra chosen, see a clean-burning flame there or the bright, expansive sun. Imagine that the consciousness in these elements of fire also have a desire to come to your aid and ignite the core of who you are. They will burn away what is not needed. Have faith that this spiritual fire knows. Set a timer for five or ten minutes and invoke its healing power with these words:

» Fire Mantra

Om Agni Devaya Namaha
"Om uhg-NEE day-VAI-yuh NAH-mah-hah"

» Sun Mantra

Om Sri Suryaya Namaha
"*Om SHREE soor-YAI-yuh NAH-mah-hah*"

Both mantras begin and end, as many traditional mantras do, with important words: the holy and primordial sound of *om*, said to be the vibration at the center of the universe, and *namaha*, which means to bow and to honor. Agni Deva is the god of fire in Hinduism. Sri, in this case, means auspicious and revered. Surya is the god of the sun. Most Sanskrit words like these have layers upon layers of deep meaning and symbology, more than we can review here. What is important is that you aim to open your body and attention to feel the power in the sounds and that you endeavor to do that with your direct experience of fire. As in the first practice, intentionally guide the sounds into your belly and even chant the mantras from there until your time is up. Notice, again, how you feel.

PRACTICE

INTUITING A PERSONAL MANTRA

Creating a personal mantra in your native language or a language other than Sanskrit can be deeply meaningful. While these phrases may not take advantage of the spiritual technology of Sanskrit, they can still function as tools to break patterns of thought by swapping in positive thought-forms where habitual states of mind used to be.

In this sense they are like affirmations. But personal mantras are more direct, simple, and rhythmic than affirmations. They strategically bypass personal identity structures rather than invoking new qualities to live into. In this way it's been my experience that personal mantras do not come from my planning mind but surface spontaneously when I am actively engaging in healing.

I have lacked determination, discrimination, and willpower for much of my life. These are classic third chakra issues, and I have found that useful mantras come to me when I am hiking or working out, actively engaging my core. In the rhythm of my stride on the gravel or the treadmill, I begin to hear supportive words. If I can capture a phrase whizzing by, I'll write it down and start rolling it over in my mind, finding a rhythm and additional words that make it more potent.

Two mantras have been very powerful for igniting my willpower. The first—"I am; I can; I will"—came to me on a long bike ride. The other arose while I was taking a scary hike through bear country. I had seen many signs of bears and my fear was growing. Then I felt my third chakra activating, and the sound *th*, as in "third," came to my mind. I began to sound it out, and then words started to come too: I heard "thorough, thorough, thorough, through." It was a rhythmic phrase that engaged my core, guided me to scan the territory more thoroughly, and instilled confidence that I would get through the situation.

These phrases have become companions of mine, and I still repeat them over and over again. They do something deeply personal for me. I feel my mind becoming clear and my belly engaging, digesting all the doubting thoughts that have been circulating.

Now it's your turn. As you engage with the other practices in this book, and as you feel your solar plexus coming online, notice words that kindle your inner flame and add a spark to your soul. Write them down. Listen to your inner stirrings. You seek a word or phrase that encapsulates an expressed third chakra. If a word is not right, don't force it. It may be as simple as "yes," or perhaps something like "I bow to the fire within me." I am asking you to use your intuition and not your mind, which can be challenging. Allow something to come through. Most importantly, trust your gut.

Once you have a personal mantra, practice with it just as you did for the first two practices, and then take it on the road. While you are in a healing cycle centered around your third chakra, utilize your personal mantra: sing it in your car, whisper it in the garden, meditate on it in a shifting subway car, or yell it at the top of your lungs in bear country.

SUMMARY

Mantras are not mere slogans but powerful tools for clearing, enhancing, and protecting the mind. While traditional mantras in the Sanskrit language have special and inherent power, all mantras give the mind a positive thoughtform to grasp onto. In this way, you can learn to use mantra to counteract the mind's tendency to endlessly chatter and bring those errant thoughts back to your core, which is such an important skill in our modern and distracted world.

Incorporating mantras skillfully into your daily life can bring great benefit in the areas where you apply them. For the third chakra, the bija mantra, traditional mantras for fire and the sun, and intuitive personal mantras will all be supportive. May these sacred and ancient practices become powerful and beloved companions on your journey of healing, wholeness, and self-transformation.

12

COLORS AND SHAPES

GINA NICOLE

There are countless ways to activate and attune our third chakras so we can align with optimal living. I find using shapes and a full spectrum of beautiful colors to be both effective and delightful.

This chapter will cover:

» how to use shapes to attune
   to your third chakra

» two practices to support your third chakra

» using color to activate your third chakra

» two exercises to activate your third chakra

MY THIRD CHAKRA STORY

We can all level up our confidence and stand in our I AM presence by activating energy in the solar plexus. We do this by listening to our bodies and sparking the third chakra in joyful and colorful ways.

In fact, I've relied on my third chakra to discover my current profession, which is serving as a subtle energy medicine practitioner. There were few job titles or industries I had yet to explore until I summoned up the courage to stand with confidence in my true I AM presence (essential self), the key takeaway or gift of the third chakra. In fact, by the time I was twenty-eight, I had held twenty-plus job titles. All I really wanted, however, was to understand more about spirituality and help people.

While it took me several years, I am now confidently and happily living in my I AM presence, and I can better cope with the types of judgments that I grew up with via my upbringing in the Catholic faith. I can still hear past comments that presented negative opinions about my intuitive work. Since working with the energy of my solar plexus, I am a confident, happy energy worker who follows my inner knowing with gusto, and I can let what is untrue roll off my back.

WORKING WITH SHAPES

Let's begin by reflecting on how we can use shapes to activate the power of the solar plexus chakra in everyday life.

Although we can use many shapes to empower activations, there are four shapes I have found both easy to apply and helpful for supporting the third chakra.

Sun and Rays

BENEFITS: The shape of the sun is commonly associated with the solar plexus chakra. It is a symbol that empowers the fire element and symbolizes positive charge, vitality, confidence, life, clarity, and bright ideas. The sun is a gift from nature, entirely outside our control yet feeding our life while offering a beautiful lesson in surrendering power.

VISUALLY: Imagine the sun shape around you, surrounding, protecting, and emanating from you.

QUALITIES WHEN OVERUSED: Arrogance, vanity, fear.

Inverted Triangle

BENEFITS: The symbol of the upside-down triangle has multiple meanings for various groups of people. It can symbolize the female reproductive organs, femininity, female empowerment, gay pride, balance, and positivity. It is about empowerment and is a symbol that encourages us to stand in our I AM presence.

VISUALLY: Pictorially, an inverted triangle looks like an arrow pointing to the lower chakras and the pathway of spiraling energy that moves through the solar plexus. Imagine this movement of energy in your mind.

QUALITIES WHEN OVERUSED: Overly materialistic, being too passive.

Ten-Petaled Lotus

BENEFITS: As Cyndi mentioned in part 1, the yantra of the third chakra is a downward-pointing triangle within a circle, which is the basis of the ten-petaled lotus. The petals on the ten-petaled lotus can be symbolic of the ten petals in the solar plexus chakra as well as the following ten aspects we must overcome to align the solar plexus: spiritual ignorance, fear, jealousy, betrayal, shame, desire, disgust, delusion, foolishness, and sadness. The petals also represent the number of nadis (energy channels) converging at the center of the solar plexus.

VISUALLY: In your mind's eye, picture this lotus in the body or in a chakra where you want to release negativity. You can also imagine yourself writing one of the ten aspects you want to transform, such as fear or jealousy, inside this shape. Of course, you can draw it too. Now request that this negative quality be energetically altered for you.

QUALITIES WHEN OVERUSED: Overconfidence, perfectionism, temptation.

Tetrahedron

BENEFITS: Personal drive, empowerment, and passion can all be brought in with the symbolism of the tetrahedron. This four-sided shape connects us to the element of fire and is one of the five platonic solids. The solar plexus is the source of our personal power, and the tetrahedron is a fire symbol. When these are unified, this activates fire in our power center (belly), helping us succeed at what we wish to accomplish.

VISUALLY: Psychically see this four-sided shape in your third chakra whenever you need to activate personal or positional power. You should immediately feel more confident.

QUALITIES WHEN OVERUSED: Overdoing, difficulty satiating, inflammation.

ATTUNEMENT WITH ACTIVATED FIRE

Since the fire element is connected to the third chakra, it is helpful to link fire and shapes when working with this chakra's subtle energy.

First, select the shape from the above list that best suits your purpose. You can choose more than one. You'll need a candle and a way to light it and some waxed paper.

Trace the selected shape on the waxed paper with a pointed object or your fingernail. You might use the thumbnail, as the thumb is associated with the third chakra. Then light the candle and feel, sense, know, and, if possible, visualize the energy of the shape moving from the fire to your solar plexus. Affirm the outcome of what you want to create while looking at the shape in the paper and imagining that this fire is enflaming your third chakra. Simultaneously say an affirmation in the present tense to help actualize the intention such as:

I am confidence. I stand in my I AM
presence and my inner knowing.

ACTIVATE EMPOWERMENT
AND RELEASE FEAR

You can use a ten-petaled lotus with an inverted triangle in the center to activate the energy in the solar plexus and release any dense aspects. When the petals of a lotus point outward, it is symbolic of the opening of a chakra. Use this symbolism while envisioning the ten petals of your third chakra opening with confidence and joy. While you are picturing this, you can internally or externally state an affirmation like this:

> *I am empowered to be who I was born to be.*
> *I transmute and open to optimal confidence,*
> *self-esteem, and clear knowing.*

There is no right or wrong in this practice and no rules. Play in the symbolism and try different combinations to see how they work for you.

WORKING WITH COLOR

Another fun and powerful way to activate and attune your third chakra is with color. The third chakra is commonly associated with yellow, which is known to increase confidence, help us stand in our power, live with self-esteem, and spark motivation.

It's fun to think outside the box and play with the full color spectrum. Color is energy, and energy is color. All colors interact with each chakra. In my experience, the human collective has access to oneness, which means that every individual is every color, and every chakra is reflected in each of the other chakras. Having said that, four colors are especially helpful for third chakra work.

As we examine the meaning of the four most powerful third chakra colors, pay attention to the various representations, meanings, and optional support. I have also shared suggestions on how you can use each color to activate and attune the third chakra.

Yellow

BENEFITS: Yellow supports us in embodying our power and confidently standing in our truth. The color symbolizes energy and ideas. Yellow connects the fire element to the symbol of the sun. It is a joyful color with a sense of knowing and happiness.

QUALITIES WHEN OVERUSED: Feeding fear, control issues, digestive issues.

SAMPLE AFFIRMATION: *Yellow ignites the energy of fire and sun, sparking my life with confidence and fun.*

Gold

BENEFITS: Gold is a color of harmony that provides soothing vibrations. It sparks confidence in our inner knowing and brings cleansing. The shine of gold offers an important solar plexus reminder to shine as brightly as the sun every day.

QUALITIES WHEN OVERUSED: Distrust, selfishness.

SAMPLE AFFIRMATION: *My light shines bright and bold; I stand in my I AM surrounded by gold.*

Red

BENEFITS: Red can activate the fire element of the solar plexus. It can be called on to promote safety as we stand in our truth and follow our inner knowing.

QUALITIES WHEN OVERUSED: Too much fire, aggressiveness, inflammation (best not to use if autoimmune challenges are present).

SAMPLE AFFIRMATION: *I am safe to be who I was born to be; red helps me passionately and confidently be me.*

Black

BENEFITS: Psychologically, black represents many aspects of the solar plexus, such as control, power, and discipline. While black is a color I scan for to identify discord in a client's energy field, it also helps absorb what is not working. Black can be helpful to use at the solar plexus to absorb subtle energy from debris that negatively impacts our confidence and power. If you imagine black removing or absorbing harmful energy, picture yourself filling that space with bright light when that step is finished.

QUALITIES WHEN OVERUSED: Concealing, too much shadow.

SAMPLE AFFIRMATION: *All discord is absorbed with black; I am empowered and do not hold back.*

Using color at the third chakra can illuminate joy and confidence. There are several ways to play with color to increase your third chakra's effectiveness.

> » Select a desirable color and add it as an accessory in your home, decor, or clothes.

» Combine the color/s chosen with shapes. For instance, you can buy a yellow pillow with a sun shape on it to increase your joy.

» Employ healing stones and crystals. Remember that the third chakra is called the "city of jewels." Select gemstones that make you feel empowered and happy, and place them in any room or on an altar. Take note of how you feel when placing the gemstones. Check if they feel and look good to you. I recommend placing a bright yellow healing stone in the center of your home, one of the prominent inlets of energy.

» Activate self-worth and your I AM presence by using feng shui. It is especially useful to address your home's "fame and reputation" section. In feng shui, this spot is found by superimposing a nine-square tic-tac-toe–like grid over the floor plan and locating the back center area; this is the space of your self-worth and the center of your power. This area represents the energy of how others see you and, most importantly, how you see yourself.

» You can activate this area by putting accessories in it that are fiery colors (red, yellow, or even purple) or using objects there in shapes that feel empowering. Since this is an area of the fire element, I would also recommend eliminating or removing water elements in colors, such as black, dark grays, and blues, because water puts out fire.

» And at any time, attune your third chakra by visualizing, sensing, or calling into yourself any shape or color that seems like it would be helpful. For example, imagine yellow if you want to activate a feeling of worth and confidence. To feel more fire, picture red. Most importantly, have fun and give your solar plexus the best gift of all—trust yourself and let your truth shine outward.

SUMMARY

Almost everything in this world is composed of shape and color. Your third chakra—home of power and mentality—is very responsive to some of the unusual shapes covered in this chapter, such as the inverted triangle, and to colors including yellow, red, black, and gold. Play with visualization and placement of colors and shapes to bring forward your super-powered self.

13

RECIPES

The third or solar plexus chakra, also called the navel chakra—or, as I like to call it, my "gut chakra"—acts as the body's physical energy center. This chakra governs the stomach and other digestive organs, such as the spleen, kidneys, stomach, liver, and pancreas, and all the processes needed for healthy digestion. This important chakra allows energy to flow, creating sustainable power for your physical health. It is also associated with self-esteem, personal identity, purpose, the individual will, and metabolism.

Are you feeling a bit low on energy or is your digestion a little sluggish? Yellow foods are where it's at if you want to boost your vitality and improve digestion.

CHOOSING YELLOW

I *love* yellow foods. I can't say no to a delectable banana or a cup of hot ginger tea. I am a sucker for ripe yellow tomatoes with a bit of flaky finishing salt. Yum. I'm sure you have your favorite yellow foods too.

When I became vegan many moons ago, choosing to eat only plant-based foods, I learned how to "eat the rainbow," meaning how to eat diversely from all the colors of foods found in nature. I didn't know it then, but that was not only a smart and healthy choice; it also assisted my chakras. Once I became more attuned to the energetics of foods and of life itself, food choices had more impact on my overall health and well-being.

So let's explore yellow foods for a moment, and then I'll share three of my favorite solar plexus chakra recipes.

Following is a partial list of some of the foods that balance the third chakra and are predominantly yellow:

» corn

» yellow potato

» pineapple

» yellow pepper

» bananas

» yellow kiwi

- » ginger
- » yellow beets
- » summer squash
- » yellow fig
- » lemons
- » yellow tomato
- » yellow lentils
- » yellow split peas

Aside from feeding the third chakra its favorite color, it's also beneficial to nourish this chakra with complex carbohydrates and whole grains such as brown rice, spelt, rye, farro, oats, beans, and sprouted grains. These foods provide crucial fiber and boost your bodily energy.

Remember, when you're deciding what foods to eat, flexibility and diversity are critical. Don't hesitate to expand your meal choices, try new foods and recipes, and be creative when preparing your meals.

RECIPES

The following yellow-based meals will diversify your home menu options and help you maintain an energetic solar plexus chakra. Here I offer one delectable plant-based recipe each for breakfast, lunch, and dinner.

Gut-Love Smoothie

SERVES 1

With this tasty breakfast drink, go for good gut health and support your digestion as well as your third chakra.

> ½ cup diced fresh pineapple (frozen will work
>   if fresh is unavailable)
> 2 frozen bananas, coarsely chopped
> Juice of ¼ lemon
> 1 small piece of peeled fresh ginger (add to taste)
> ¾ cup plant-based milk or coconut water of choice
> ½ cup ice cubes*
> Golden syrup, optional and to taste (I like Lyle's
>   Golden Syrup, available online and at many
>   grocery stores) or another natural sweetener

*If you're using frozen fruit, reduce or eliminate the ice cubes depending on the desired consistency.

Place the chopped pineapple in a blender. Add the frozen bananas, lemon juice, ginger, and plant-based milk of your choice. Add the ice cubes if using. Add the golden syrup to taste, if using (I add roughly two teaspoons). Blend until smooth and serve cold.

Anthony's aMAIZEing Third Chakra Salad

SERVES 2

You'll love this salad—and so will everyone you know, vegan or not.

- 2 tablespoons avocado oil
- 5 to 6 ears freshly shucked corn or 4 cups frozen
- ¼ teaspoon chili powder
- ¼ teaspoon smoked paprika
- ¼ teaspoon smoked sea salt
- 1 garlic clove, crushed
- 1 tablespoon freshly squeezed lemon juice (more if desired)
- 3 tablespoons vegan mayonnaise (I am a big fan of the Vegenaise brand)
- ¼ yellow onion, diced
- 1 yellow pepper, thinly sliced
- 1 chili pepper, thinly sliced (I like the Buist's Yellow Cayenne variety, but any other pepper, mild or spicy, will work)
- ¼ cup chopped cilantro
- ¼ cup crumbled vegan feta, optional

Heat the avocado oil in a large skillet over high heat. Once it's hot, add the corn to the skillet. Allow the corn to brown for about five minutes; you don't need to stir it. Once it's browned, stir the corn well and add the chili powder, paprika, salt, and garlic. Cook for another minute until the mixture is fragrant.

Transfer the corn mixture to a large bowl. Add the lemon juice, mayonnaise, onion, yellow pepper, and chili pepper. Toss to combine and mix well.

Add the fresh cilantro and feta, if using, and stir again. Taste and adjust salt. Serve immediately or refrigerate until ready to serve.

NOTE: You can roast the ears of corn first if you like. Allow them to cool before removing the kernels from the cob. This delicious salad can be served hot or cold. If eating raw is your jam, you can also make this salad without cooking the corn, using fresh or thawed frozen corn.

Mellow Yellow Split Pea Soup

SERVES 2

If you're seeking extra healing power for your solar plexus chakra, I suggest adding yellow spices like turmeric, ginger, or cumin to your dishes for added impact.

> 1 tablespoon avocado or coconut oil
>
> 1 yellow onion, chopped
>
> 1 yellow pepper, diced
>
> 3 cloves garlic, minced
>
> 6 cups vegetable broth
>
> 1 cup yellow split peas
>
> 1 large yellow potato, peeled and chopped
>
> Kernels from 5 ears of corn (about 2½ cups)
>
> ¾ teaspoon smoked paprika
>
> 1 teaspoon sea salt plus more to taste
>
> ¾ cup coconut cream
>
> 1½ tablespoons apple cider vinegar
>
> Chopped chives or parsley for garnish, optional

Heat the oil in a large pot over medium heat. Add the onion and pepper and cook, stirring occasionally, for a few minutes, until the onion is translucent. Add the garlic and cook, stirring constantly, until fragrant. Stir in the broth, split peas, potato, corn, paprika, and salt, and bring the mixture to a boil over high heat. Lower the heat, cover the pot, and simmer for about 45 minutes, stirring occasionally, until the split peas are tender. To thicken the soup, puree it partially with an immersion blender or put about half the soup in a food processor, puree it, and return it to the pot. Stir in the coconut cream and apple cider vinegar. Adjust the seasonings for your taste buds. Serve hot and garnish with chives if using.

PART 2: SUSAN WEIS-BOHLEN

Off and on throughout my life, I have felt the heavy weight of important things in my gut, the area of the solar plexus chakra. Power or lack thereof, possessions or the missing of them, wanting more or less of this or that. Constantly lurking in my gut were doubt, insecurity, and pain; greed too.

The third chakra is the home of belief systems, including the thought that we must have *more* if we are to feel secure. Think about whether you really need more money, objects, a bigger house, or more friends. Maybe what's vital is to dig deeper and see what is really going on in that shining yellow orb that attracts so much attention.

You may hear the third chakra speaking to you and choose to ignore it, but messages of truth are always emanating from deep within it, waiting to be heard, weighed, and balanced. *I'm hungry. I'm thirsty. I need attention.* With discernment, you can sort these from the mixed messages you grew up with—for example, that you should hold in your stomach so it looks flatter. Your solar plexus suggests *I should just be myself instead.*

When sitting quietly in meditation or contemplation, you can discern the needs, wants, and desires of the gemfire chakra more clearly. Evaluate for the deepest need. It might not be food and drink; your inner self could be seeking another kind of nourishment. Becoming more familiar with this chakra will help you decipher its messages and impulses.

In Ayurveda, the ancient Indian system of science and living that I practice, we access the potential healing effects of foods through their initial taste as well as their after-effects in the gut. This is one way to balance the mind and body, and it involves a type of alchemy: for example, some foods, like onion, can be pungent when raw but sweet when cooked and thus have different healing qualities in each state. Intuitively ask your body what version is best for you right now.

The food and drink in this chapter support your healthiest decisions to nourish and care for your third chakra. But before you enter the kitchen to rustle up foods that will support your solar plexus chakra, check in with all the other tools in this book to evaluate this chakra's current state. Is it a raging fire, as when we're ego-driven and on overdrive? Or is it hesitant, apprehensive, in need of boosting? You will find recipe choices here to balance and calm the beast or light your fire.

Third Chakra Smoothie

SERVES 1

The fruits and oil in this recipe are filled with vitamins and minerals to boost the immune system and clear the path to activate the third chakra's natural desires. This recipe will promote balance in the chakra by nourishing the tissues.

> 1 medium banana, sliced
> 1 cup diced cantaloupe
> ½ cup pineapple juice
> ¼ cup orange juice
> ½ cup whole fat coconut milk (room temperature from the can or box)
> 1 tablespoon honey
> 1 teaspoon powdered turmeric
> 1 teaspoon flaxseed oil

Place all the ingredients in a blender and mix until smooth. Drink immediately or store in an airtight container in the fridge for no more than twelve hours. Enjoy this golden-yellow power drink on an empty stomach, and don't eat solid food afterward until you feel hungry or for at least one hour.

Charred Lemon Garbanzo Bean Bonanza

SERVES 2

Garbanzo beans (chickpeas) are considered light and drying in Ayurveda. The lemon in this recipe is pungent and bright, and the bitter greens and herbs are detoxifying and refreshing. All in all, this recipe illuminates the senses with its vibrant colors and surprising flavors, sparking creativity with a playfulness to lighten your mood and open you up to unlimited possibilities. I love this for breakfast or lunch or on a scoop of rice, quinoa, or pasta for dinner. Enjoy this meal when you're feeling a lack of desire or intention. It will fire you up.

> 1 whole lemon, sliced in half and charred
>   (preparation instructions below)
> 1½ cups cooked dried garbanzo beans
>   or canned beans (see note)
> 10 yellow grape tomatoes, sliced in half
> ¼ cup thinly sliced red onion
> ½ cup canned corn, drained, or steamed frozen corn
> 1 tablespoon organic extra virgin olive oil
> ½ teaspoon cumin powder
> ½ teaspoon cumin seeds
> 1 tablespoon grated ginger
> Salt and pepper to taste
> Handful each chopped parsley, cilantro,
>   and feta cheese for garnish

NOTE: If you're using canned garbanzos, save half the liquid (called *aqua fava*, or bean water) to add later. If you're cooking dried beans, reserve about a half cup of the cooking water.

PREPARE THE CHARRED LEMON: Heat a cast-iron pan over medium-high heat. Slice the lemon in half and rub a small amount of olive oil on the cut ends of the halves to ensure they won't stick to the pan. Test the heat of the pan by sprinkling a few drops of water on the surface; when the water sizzles, it's hot enough. Place the lemon halves pulp-side down in the pan and leave them undisturbed until you can smell the lemon charring, about three to five minutes. Remove them immediately. Charring the lemon makes it sweeter and reduces the acid, which makes it more digestible. It also brings out incredible flavor and enhances all the other ingredients.

In a medium-sized bowl, mix together the garbanzos, tomatoes, red onion, corn, olive oil, cumin powder, cumin seeds, ginger, and salt and pepper to taste. Squeeze the juice of half the charred lemon into the bean mixture along with the reserved bean water and stir to combine. Allow the mixture to sit at room temperature for about fifteen minutes for all the flavors to meld. To garnish, thinly slice the remaining lemon half, place the slices on top, and sprinkle with the parsley, cilantro, and feta.

Golden Sweet Pepper Stew

SERVES 2

This perfect side dish of bright yellow peppers turns unbelievably sweet, with just enough pungency from the garlic and herbs for balance. Pair this stew with seared yellowfin tuna (see page 206) for the perfect solar plexus meal. This recipe cooks up well in a Dutch oven, but if you don't have one, a large pot with a tight-fitting lid will work too.

> ¾ cup organic extra virgin olive oil, divided
> 6 medium or 8 small garlic cloves,
>   peeled and thinly sliced
> 1 large yellow onion, thinly sliced
> 4 to 6 yellow bell peppers, deseeded
>   and cut into ½-inch strips
> ½ cup crushed tomatoes (canned works well)
> Small handful dried or fresh oregano, thyme, or basil
> Flaky salt (such as Maldon sea salt)
>   and black pepper to taste
> 1 tablespoon white wine vinegar or citrus vinegar (buy
>   ready-made or see the note below to make your own)

Add a half cup of the olive oil to a Dutch oven or other pot over medium heat. When it begins to shimmer, toss in the garlic and mix well. Keep stirring until the garlic is just golden, ensuring that it does not burn (two to three minutes). Add the onion slices and coat them well with the oil and garlic mixture. Cook until the onions become translucent. Add the peppers to the pot, mix well, and cook, stirring every few minutes until they begin to cook down and soften. This should take about twenty minutes.

Add the crushed tomato and herbs and stir. After heating the mixture for a few minutes, lower the heat to a simmer and cook for about 1 hour, stirring occasionally. If the ingredients begin to stick to the pot, add just enough water to avoid sticking and stir well. When the peppers are very soft, remove the stew from the heat. Stir in the rest of the olive oil. Add salt and pepper to taste and then the vinegar. This dish is great hot, warm, or chilled.

NOTE: To make your own citrus vinegar, heat two cups of distilled white vinegar on the stove. Remove it from the heat and add two or three cups of the zest and/or peels of any citrus fruit, such as lemon, lime, oranges, or grapefruit. Allow the blend to cool, pour it into a clean glass jar, and seal it. Allow the vinegar to sit for fifteen to thirty days to infuse. As an added bonus, you can use this mix for cleaning.

Seared Tuna

SERVES 2

12 ounces wild-caught yellowfin tuna

2 tablespoons white sesame seeds

1 teaspoon chopped garlic or ½ teaspoon garlic powder

1 teaspoon chopped fresh ginger root or
½ teaspoon powdered ginger

1 teaspoon toasted sesame seed oil

1 teaspoon untoasted sesame seed oil
plus extra for cooking

Squeeze of lemon juice

Mix the sesame seeds, garlic, ginger, and one teaspoon each of the toasted and untoasted sesame oils in a bowl. Press the tuna into this mixture and coat it well on both sides. Heat a skillet over high heat, add enough untoasted sesame oil to cover the cooking area, and sear the tuna for about thirty seconds on each side. Plate it along with the golden sweet pepper stew and add a squeeze of lemon.

CONCLUSION

You began your journey by peering at the sun. I encouraged you to gaze at the ball of light in the sky, if only in your imagination. Then you were invited to behold the sparkling, flaming jewel within your solar plexus: your third chakra, your own personal sun filled with light and love.

My hope is that as you journeyed through this book, you befriended this brilliant gemfire energy center, called *manipura* in Sanskrit. If so, you've experienced many gains already, and you can return to these chapters again and again to tease out even more.

A bubbling sphere of mental and intellectual activity, this chakra also governs vital physical functions, including many aspects of your digestion and immune and neurological systems. We could all use improvement in these areas. Within its chalice bubbles a yellow energy that invigorates your journey toward success and well-being. Humming its *bija,* or seed syllable, of *Ram*, you learned how to access a universe of knowledge and apply it to your everyday life.

Throughout part 1 you engaged many of the traditional benefits of interacting with your solar plexus chakra. Whether accessing the major god, goddess, seed carrier, or another guide, you opened to the heavenly realms that are available through this beam of light. Aflame with the fire element associated with this chakra, you lit your mind from within. You even touched into the red energy of the kundalini, the feminine serpent that can ignite so many areas of your life. You did so much more as well before turning the page for the next odyssey.

In part 2 you expanded your ability to meet yourself in your solar plexus through exciting and adventurous avenues of personal growth. Think of the sparkle you will add to your life as you explore your newfound relationships with spirit allies, yoga exercises, body awareness activities, meditations, vibrational remedies, sound techniques, cooking experiences, and so much more.

Ponder how you will continue to fuel the torch of your solar plexus chakra. Choices include work, relationships, enjoyment, or learning. The possibilities are endless, as is the light that you are.

© Katie Cannon Photography

ANTHONY J. W. BENSON serves as a creative business strategist, manager, coach, producer, and writer specializing in working with consciously awake authors, speakers, musicians, entrepreneurs, and small and large businesses. He has shared his expertise on numerous podcasts and radio and television shows. Anthony has led a mindful plant-based lifestyle for over 35 years.

ANTHONYJWBENSON.COM
INJOICREATIVE.COM

© Atkin Photographics

JO-ANNE BROWN is an intuitive, energy healer, and author who lives in central Queensland, Australia, with a background including engineering and bioresonance therapy. She helps highly sensitive people find meaning in their profound emotional experiences and release disharmonious patterns. She is featured in the internationally bestselling multi-author book *Intuitive: Speaking Her Truth*.

JOANNEINTUITIVE.COM

© Dear Davian Photography

LINDSAY FAUNTLEROY is a licensed acupuncturist and founder of The Spirit Seed, a school that offers personal and professional development courses that are rooted in ancestral understandings of health, humanity, nature, and the cosmos. Lindsay is a certified instructor for the National Certification Commission for Acupuncture and Oriental Medicine (NCCAOM), as well as a facilitator of the Flower Essence Society's global practitioner certification program.

OCEANSANDDRIVERS.COM
THESPIRITSEED.ORG/INOURELEMENTBOOK

© Michelle Francesconi

AMANDA HUGGINS is an anxiety and mindfulness coach, certified yoga instructor, podcast host, author, and speaker. Her signature "Scientific, Spiritual, Practical" approach has helped thousands achieve transformation in mind, body, and soul. Besides presenting online courses, Amanda offers guidance on her podcast, *Anxiety Talks with Amanda*, and has an online community of over a half million followers.

INSTAGRAM AND TIKTOK @ITSAMANDAHUGGINS
AMANDAHUGGINSCOACHING.COM

MARGARET ANN LEMBO is the author of *The Essential Guide to Crystals, Chakra Awakening, Animal Totems and the Gemstone Kingdom, The Essential Guide to Aromatherapy and Vibrational Healing, Angels and Gemstone Guardians Cards, Gemstone Guardians and Your Soul Purpose*, among other titles. She is an award-winning aromatherapist and the owner of The Crystal Garden, the conscious living store and center of the Palm Beaches.

MARGARETANNLEMBO.COM
THECRYSTALGARDEN.COM

GINA NICOLE is a feng shui consultant, subtle energy medicine practitioner, and the author of a deck of wisdom cards. She encourages empathic people to orient their minds, bodies, spirits, and homes to align with higher frequencies to make impeccably clear and intuitive decisions. She loves to travel and is devoted to bringing transformational light to the foster care system.

GINANICOLE.NET

BLAKE TEDDER is a yoga instructor, musician, and guide who helps people connect to life and health by holding sacred spaces with movement, ritual, sound, and song. He hosts a podcast with yoga legends Angela Farmer and Victor van Kooten, a weekly radio show exploring contemplative musical landscapes, and, formerly, the internationally acclaimed *Full Lotus Kirtan Show*. He writes songs and leads chanting groups when not attending to his full-time work for a university research forest.

BLAKETEDDER.COM

AMELIA VOGLER is an energy medicine and grounding specialist, internationally respected teacher of energy medicine, spiritual coach, and meditation guide. She embeds essential energetic practices in her meditations and teachings to better humanity. Maintaining an international private practice, she has helped thousands of individuals transform through grounding practices, intuitive insight, and advanced energy medicine.

AMELIAVOGLER.COM
VOGLERINSTITUTE.COM

SUSAN WEIS-BOHLEN is certified in Ayurveda from the Chopra Center and has studied with Dr. Vasant Lad and Amadea Morningstar. She has also served on the National Ayurvedic Medical Association (NAMA) Board of Directors since 2018. A former bookstore owner, Susan is also the author of *Ayurveda Beginner's Guide: Essential Ayurvedic Principles and Practices to Balance and Heal Naturally* and *Seasonal Self-Care Rituals: Eat, Breathe, Move, and Sleep Better—According to Your Dosha.*

BREATHEAYURVEDA.COM

TO WRITE TO THE AUTHOR

If you wish to contact the author or would like more information about this book, please write to the author in care of Llewellyn Worldwide and we will forward your request. Both the author and the publisher appreciate hearing from you and learning of your enjoyment of this book and how it has helped you. Llewellyn Worldwide cannot guarantee that every letter written to the author can be answered, but all will be forwarded. Please write to:

Cyndi Dale
Llewellyn Worldwide
2143 Wooddale Drive
Woodbury, MN 55125-2989

Please enclose a self-addressed stamped envelope for reply or $1.00 to cover costs. If outside the USA, enclose an international postal reply coupon.

• • • • • •

Many of Llewellyn's authors have websites with additional information and resources. For more information, please visit our website:

WWW.LLEWELLYN.COM